# CIRCULAR WALKS
# IN THE VALE OF GLAMORGAN

# Circular Walks in the Vale of Glamorgan

Dorothy Hamilton

ISBN: 0-86381-603-7

Cover design: Alan Jones

First published in 2000 by
Gwasg Carreg Gwalch, 12 Iard yr Orsaf, Llanrwst, Wales LL26 0EH
☎ 01492 642031    ▤ 01492 641502
✆ books@carreg-gwalch.co.uk    Web site: www.carreg-gwalch.co.uk

# Contents

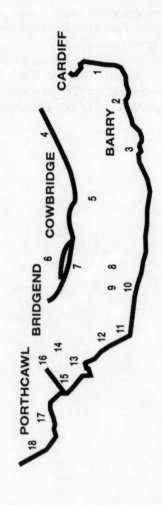

# VALE OF GLAMORGAN
## Location of the walks

PORTHCAWL

BRIDGEND

COWBRIDGE

CARDIFF

BARRY

# Introduction

The walks in this guide to the Vale of Glamorgan are 5-12 kilometres long. The walks selected highlight the area's spectacular coastline, beautiful rolling countryside and historical interest.

All the walks have sketch maps and easy to follow directions. The starting points are at, or near, a car park or parking place. Directions are given to reach the start by car and public transport.

The routes are graded as easy or moderate according to length and terrain. None of the routes are strenuous: uphill sections are usually short. The average amount of time that is needed to complete each walk is given, but extra time may be needed for picnics, photography, bird watching, looking around historical sites etc. Adequate route descriptions are given to complete all walks without referring to other maps but, for those who like to carry one, all the routes can be found on OS Explorer 1:25,000 No. 151. Points of interest are included for each walk, and these give background information relating to the landscape, historic sites and legends of the area. Facilities list alternative parking, public toilets, cafes, pubs, nearby campsites and places to visit.

Finally, a cautionary note. Care must be taken on cliff and beach walks on this stretch of coast, especially if there are children in the group. The cliffs are prone to rock falls and it is dangerous to walk or stand close to cliff edges. It is also risky to walk directly beneath the cliffs. The Bristol Channel has the second highest tidal range in the world and incoming tides move rapidly – check the tide is going out before walking along beaches or crossing to Sully Island (*Ynys Sili*).

## Background

Geographically, the Vale of Glamorgan – Bro Morgannwg – is the lowland area stretching between Cardiff (*Caerdydd*) and Port

Talbot. Bordering the sea, it is not a valley, but an uplifted coastal plateau of limestone and younger rocks. The Welsh name 'Bro', meaning region or area, is therefore more accurate than the English 'Vale'.

This is a fertile, green, agricultural landscape, drained by small rivers. The Vale meets the Bristol Channel at a line of cliffs, which are kept near vertical by frequent rock falls. Beneath the cliffs there is often a low platform of rocks, rich in fossils. Towards the western end of the Vale, large tracts of land have been overlain by sand dunes.

During the geological Carboniferous era warm shallow seas covered the area with reefs and numerous sea creatures, whose remains contributed to the formation of Carboniferous limestone. Later there were coastal swamps, the origin of present-day coal measures. This period was followed by a stage of mountain building and later, erosion. During Jurassic times clear seas again covered the land. This was the period when the beautiful blue-grey limestone and darker shales of the cliffs that we see today were formed.

There followed another period of earth movements during which the Alps were uplifted, and this pressure created the upfolds and downfolds in the strata along the Glamorgan coast. South Wales emerged as a land mass followed by the sea retreating across the Vale of Glamorgan, and forming the present-day platform, about 60 metres above the present sea level.

During the Ice Ages the sea level fell, and at times the South Wales Ice Cap may have reached the coast. When the ice began to thaw, torrents of water cut deep valleys, extending to what is now the Bristol Channel. Examples are Cwm Col-huw and Cwm Marcroes.

The first men probably came into the Vale of Glamorgan during a warm period of the last Ice Age. An estimation of Britain's total population during the Palaeolithic – interglacial, Old Stone Age – era is 500. Only a small number would have lived in South Wales. However, bones and stone artefacts dating back more than 30,000 years have been found in caves on the Gower peninsula. Evidence of New Stone Age Man comes from Neolithic tombs. They are of the type known as *Severn – Cotswold*, and Tinkinswood (Walk 4) is an outstanding example. Neolithic people cleared the dense woodland and farmed, grazing animals and growing crops.

The Bronze Age (2000-1000BC) was a period of population explosion, and more clearance of woodland. Burial custom changed from communal to individual cremated burial in pottery vessels. Standing stones belong to this period. Implements from the late Bronze Age have been found around Llantwit Major *(Llanilltud Fawr)* and Cardiff.

Celtic tribes from Central Europe reached the Vale about the 6th century BC, the start of the Iron Age. They constructed hill forts along the coast. They can be seen on Walks 2, 3, 10, 12 and 13. Because the cliffs were defended on the seaward side by impassable cliffs, artificial defences were only needed on the inland sides. The banks were built of earth, stone and rubble. These people organised themselves into the tribe known as the Silures, and it took the Romans, when they invaded Glamorgan, many years to overpower them.

Roman forts were established at Cardiff and, possibly, Cowbridge *(Y Bont-faen)*, which lay on the road from the legionary fortress at Isca *(Caerleon)* to the fort of Moridunum, at Caerfyrddin. Villas have been excavated at Ely and Llantwit Major. By the early 5th century Roman rule had come to an end.

After the Romans left there was a reassertion of Celtic culture, and a forming of separate, small kingdoms, each with a powerful king. This part of south Wales took the name Glwysing, derived from its King Glywys. In the 8th century the name changed to Morgannwg, possibly after Morgan ab Athrwys who died about 665. His descendants ruled for five hundred years. Caradog ap Gruffydd and Iestyn ap Gwrgant were the last Welsh rulers here in the 1090s.

During the 6th and 7th centuries monastic settlements were

established. The Celtic saints, Illtud and Cadog, set up monasteries at Llantwit Major *(Llanilltud Fawr)* and Llancarfan. These *clasau* would have consisted of huts for the monks, a wooden church and a cemetery within an enclosure *(llan)*. Carved stones from this period can be seen in the church at Llantwit Major *(Llanilltud Fawr)* and in Margam Stones Museum.

The first Norman ruler to cross into south Wales was William FitzOsbern, who had been made Earl of Hereford. He built keeps at Chepstow and Monmouth, and by the time he died in 1071, he had reached Usk. About 1093, Robert Fitzhamon, Lord of Gloucester, invaded Morgannwg, and Iestyn ap Gwrgant was overthrown. The Vale of Glamorgan was divided into manors. Fitzhamon kept Llantwit Major for himself and most of the others were given to his knights. Llancarfan was given to the Benedict Abbey of Gloucester. Bristol acquired the manor of Penarth. Fitzhamon probably brought some of his Anglo-Saxon tenants from the west of England with him into Glamorgan. Although many Welsh people went into the mountains of 'Blaenau Morgannwg', some remained in the Vale. Intermarriage was used to consolidate the power of both Welsh and Norman ruling houses.

The Normans built castles and fortified manor houses, and provided the new villages with churches. The later churches stand today. Monasteries were established at Ewenny and Margam. These became parish churches in the 16th century following Henry VIII's break with Rome. The local gentry bought land formerly owned by the monasteries, thus extending their estates. The Stradlings, the most important family living in the Vale, bought Monknash *(Yr As Fawr)* which had belonged to Neath Abbey *(Abaty Nedd)*. Lower down the social scale were the squires, and some of their picturesque Tudor houses survive today, such as Plas Llanmihangel (Walk 8) and Llansannor *(Llansanwyr)* Court (Walk 7). The most splendid of these buildings is Old Beaupre (Walk 6), built by the Bassetts.

The Vale prospered in the following centuries, maintaining peace when riots occurred elsewhere. After 1820 wages were said to be higher in this area than anywhere else in rural Wales or the west of England. The only flicker of dissatisfaction was when the monopoly of the established church was challenged in 1749 by the building of the first Methodist chapel at Aberthin, near Cowbridge. The Baptists built their first chapel in 1777. However, there were few Nonconformists until the mid 19th century when, over a short space of time, chapels opened in most of the larger villages. By 1851 there were three Nonconformists to every Anglican.

When Penarth and Barry became boom towns because of the docks and railways, many Vale labourers left the land. Attracted by high wages in the Vale, farm workers from the west of England and Ireland came to work during the harvests. In the mid 19th century nearly half of the inhabitants of some of the villages had been born outside Glamorgan.

Nowadays, apart from farmers, most of the population in the Vale are commuters or retired people, and their origins may be anywhere in Britain or farther afield.

Airfields and industry fringe the area, but the countryside and villages retain an air of remoteness and an especial charm. The coast between Newton *(Porthcawl)* in the west and Aberthaw in the east is completely unspoilt, protected by a Heritage Coast status.

## Welsh Place-names

The following words are sometimes used in place-names in the Vale of Glamorgan.

Aber – *estuary, river mouth*
Afal – *apple*
Afon – *river*
Bach/Fach – *small*
Bryn – *hill*
Bwlch – *gap, pass*
Cae – *field*
Caer – *fort*
Capel – *chapel*
Castell – *castle*
Celli/Gelli – *grove*
Clawdd – *hedge,
    embankment or wall*
Coch – *red*
Coed – *wood, trees*
Craig/Graig – *rock*
Croes – *cross*
Cwm – *valley*
Cwrt – *court*
Cwter/Gwter – *channel*
Dinas – *fort*
Dryw – *wren*
Eglwys – *church*
Ffordd – *road*
Ffynnon – *spring, well*
Garn – *cairn*
Glan – *river bank*

Gwyn – *white*
Isaf – *lower*
Llyn – *lake*
Maes – *field*
Mawr/Fawr – *big, great, large*
Morfa – *marsh*
Mynach – *monk*
Nant – *stream*
Newydd – *new*
Orsaf/Gorsaf – *station*
Pant – *hollow, valley*
Parc – *park, field*
Pen – *head, top*
Pentre – *village*
Perllan/Berllan – *orchard*
Plas – *mansion*
Pont – *bridge*
Porth – *port*
Pwll – *pool, pit*
Tafarn – *inn*
Traeth – *beach*
Tref – *town*
Tŷ – *house*
Uchaf – *upper*
Y/Yr – *the*
Ynys – *island*

# Information

| | |
|---|---|
| Cardiff Tourist Information Centre | 01222 227281 |
| Penarth Tourist Information Centre | 01222 708849 |
| Barry Island Tourist Information Centre | 01446 747171 |
| Llantwit Major Tourist Information Centre | 01446 796086 |
| Bridgend Tourist Information Centre | 01656 654906 |
| Porthcawl Tourist Information Centre | 01656 782211 |
| Vale of Glamorgan Tourism | 01446 709325 |
| Glamorgan Heritage Coast Centre | 01656 880157 |
| Sea Watch Centre | 01446 795203 |
| Cosmeston Lakes Country Park | 01222 701678 |
| Kenfig National Nature Reserve | 01656 743386 |
| The Flat Holm Project (Boat trips to island) | 01446 747661 |
| Fonmon Castle (Tours) | 01446 710206 |
| St Donat's Castle (Tours) | 01446 792271 |
| Dyffryn Gardens | 01222 593328 |
| Vale of Glamorgan Public Transport Unit | 01446 704687 |
| Weathercall | 0891 500409 |

# Country Code

1. Guard against any risk of fire.
2. Keep to the public rights of way when crossing farmland.
3. Avoid causing any damage to walls, fences and hedges.
4. Leave farm gates as you find them.
5. Keep dogs under control and on leads in the presence of livestock.
6. Leave machinery, farm animals and crops alone.
7. Take care not to pollute water.
8. Carry your litter home with you.
9. Protect all wildlife, plants and trees.
10. Avoid making any unnecessary noise.
11. Drive carefully on country roads.
12. Enjoy and respect the countryside.

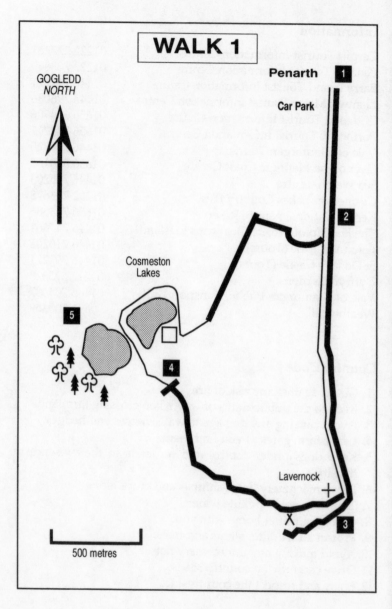

# Penarth – Lavernock (*Larnog*) – Cosmeston Lakes – Penarth

*OS Maps:*   1:50 000 Landranger Sheet 171;
             1:25 000 Explorer Sheet 151.

*Start:*     Lower Penarth, south of Penarth pier, near the start of the cliff walk. G.R. 186704.

*Access:*    Off the B4267, 5km south of the A4055. Buses from Cardiff and Barry. Trains from Cardiff.

*Parking:*   Car park near the cliff walk, signposted 800m south of Penarth pier.

*Grade:*     Easy – cliff and lakeside paths, lane.

*Time:*      2-3 hours.

## Points of Interest:

1. Penarth is often called 'the garden by the sea' because of its beautiful flower beds. Originally a small village, Penarth became a fashionable town when mine and ship owners built their houses on the headland, and an elegant seaside resort developed along the coast. The small, medieval St Augustine's church was replaced by a much grander Victorian building, designed by William Butterfield. The 200m long pier, built in 1894, suffered fire damage in 1931 when its wooden concert pavilion was destroyed. Sixteen years later, the 7000 ton Canadian steamer *Port Royal Park* hit the pier broadside during a gale. The *Waverley*, the last sea-going paddle steamer in the world, still calls at Penarth pier during the summer months. From the sea front there are views across the Bristol Channel to Somerset.

2. Flat Holm and Steep Holm are two islands composed of carboniferous limestone situated in the Bristol Channel,

between Brean Down in Somerset and Lavernock Point (*Trwyn Larnog*) in Morgannwg. Steep Holm, the higher and nearer to Somerset, has a summit over 120m above sea level. Both islands were used by Viking raiders, hence the name 'holm'. Flat Holm was once a hermitage for monks, and it is reputed that two knights who murdered the Archbishop of Canterbury, Thomas à Beckett, in 1170 are buried there. In the 1860s, Flat Holm was fortified with gun batteries as part of the coastal defence system against possible French invasion, but they were never used. The island was refortified during the Second World War with new batteries, and barracks for 350 soldiers. A cholera hospital was built on Flat Holm in 1883. Nowadays, the islands are nature reserves, supporting the rare wild leek, slow worms, and colonies of sea birds. Scheduled boat trips run from Barry Island to Flat Holm during the summer months.

3. The first wireless telegraph message ever sent across water was transmitted between Flat Holm and the farm at Lavernock Point on the 11th of May 1897. It was the achievement of Guglielmo Marconi, who had been unable to interest the Italian government in his experiments. With the help of the British Post Office and their engineers, two 33 metres high masts were built to send the simple message 'Are you ready?' Outside Lavernock church there is a plaque commemorating this event between Marconi and his partner, George Kemp. Shortly afterwards they transmitted between Lavernock and Brean Down.

4. Cosmeston village had developed in the 12th century around the manor of a Norman family, the Costentin family. Famine and the Black Death of 1348-9 devastated the village and the manor fell into ruin. Cosmeston was rediscovered in 1982 by archaeologists. The excavated buildings have been rebuilt.

5. An area of Cosmeston Lakes Country Park has been designated a Site of Special Scientific Interest (S.S.S.I.). The country park has been developed on the site of former limestone quarries. The lake on your left is a conservation area where reeds provide nesting places for birds. Swans, coot,

moorhen, mallard, great crested grebe, tufted duck and heron are the most likely birds to be spotted. In the winter look for wigeon and pochard. Reed buntings and several varieties of warblers frequent the marshland. Near the east lake there is a conservation area where orchids grow.

**Walk Directions:**                    (-) denotes Point of Interest

1. From (Lower) Penarth (1) car park walk out on to the cliffs and turn right along a surfaced path. The two islands visible in the Bristol Channel are Steep Holm and Flat Holm (2).

2. Pass some houses on the right. At the end of the houses the path becomes rougher and passes between trees and bushes. It eventually reaches a lane end at Lavernock *(Larnog)* (3)

3. Turn right and pass a church on the right. Follow the lane uphill to the B4267.

4. Cross the road to a stile. As you walk across the field you will glimpse the reconstructed village of Cosmeston (4) on your right. Cross a stile near a gate and turn right on the track.

5. Continue on the track and ignore other paths and tracks leading off it. Cross a bridge separating the Cosmeston Lakes (5) and in 40 metres turn right on a broad track.

6. Pass some picnic tables and a children's playground. Walk beside the lake to the Visitor Centre.

7. Leave the car park at the Visitor Centre by bearing left, then right to reach the B4267. Turn left on the pavement and in 400 metres pass a garage on the left. In another 80 metres turn right on a road that crosses a bridge above a disused railway. (This was the Penarth-Barry Line. It closed in 1968.)

8. At a junction bear right, then shortly left along Stanton Way. Walk ahead to reach the path along the cliffs. Turn left and retrace your steps to the start at the car park.

## Facilities:

Alternative car park at Cosmeston Lakes Country Park. Cafe, Visitor Centre and toilets in the country park. Cosmeston Medieval Village. Camp site at Lavernock. Boat trips from Penarth pier.

# Sully *(Sili)* – Old Cogan – Cosmeston Lakes Country Park – Swanbridge – Sully

| | |
|---|---|
| *OS Maps:* | 1:50 000 Landranger Sheet 171; 1:25 000 Explorer Sheet 151. |
| *Start:* | Sully Church. G.R. 150683. |
| *Access:* | Sully is on the B4267, south of the A4055 and east of Barry. The church is at the western end of the village. Buses from Barry and Cardiff. |
| *Parking:* | Near the church. |
| *Grade:* | Moderate – field paths, beach and coast path, lanes. |
| *Time:* | 3½-4 hours. Allow more time if you wish to cross (low tide only) to Sully Island *(Ynys Sili)*. |

## Points of Interest:

1. Sully dates from Norman times when the de Sully family built a castle behind where the present-day Sully Inn is situated. Only traces of the castle remain. The church of St John the Baptist is on the same site as a church founded by them. It has a 15th century tower. Sully was once a busy port and a haunt of smugglers.

2. The lovely little church of St Peter, Old Cogan, has herring-bone masonry dating back to the pre-Norman period. The western part of the nave and the south porch are 16th century. It may be the oldest church in Morgannwg.

3. The Cosmeston Lakes Country Park has been developed on the site of the Downswood limestone quarry. It operated for 80 years before closing in 1970. After its closure, underground springs created the lakes and wetlands, providing habitats for

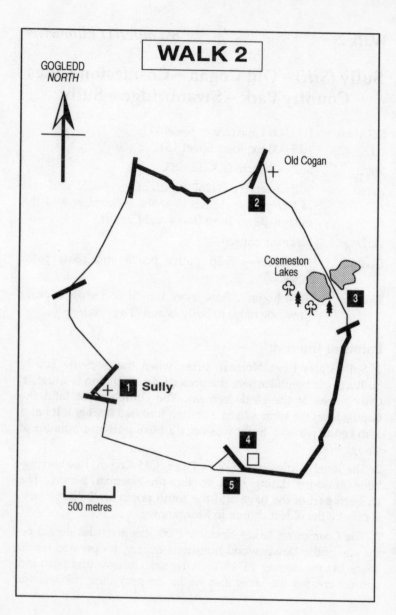

# WALK 2

GOGLEDD
*NORTH*

Old Cogan

**2**

Cosmeston
Lakes

**3**

**1** Sully

**4**

**5**

500 metres

many plant and animal species. The country park also has areas of broadleaved woodland, scrubland and meadows.

4. Near the Captain's Wife public house is the site of the old Sully House. The house was tenanted by a sea captain who traded from Sully on his own ship, sometimes accompanied by his wife. During a voyage his wife died and, because sailors are superstitious about keeping a corpse on board, he folded his wife's body and hid it in a box. When he returned to shore he buried the box behind Sully House, whilst he made arrangements for a proper coffin and burial. When he returned to dig up the box he found that the box, and his wife's body, had disappeared and neither could be found. It was thought that somebody watched him bury the box and, thinking it to be treasure, had dug it up. The lady's ghost was said to haunt the area. Many years later, when some stones were removed in the stableyard of Sully House, the doubled-up skeleton of a woman was found. The bones were buried and the ghost has not been seen since the burial. The Captain's Wife public house opened in the 1970s near the location of the old Sully House.

5. Sully Island can be reached by walking across the tidal causeway, but the crossing should only be attempted at low tide. (Consult tide timetables before crossing.) On the eastern side of the island there is a small Iron Age hill fort. About 100 years ago coins belonging to the Roman period were found on the island. Dinosaur footprints were found on the bedrock at the western end of Sully beach in the 1980s.

**Walk Directions:**                    (-) denotes Point of Interest

1. Pass Sully Church (1) nearby on your right, and bear right along the road to pass the Sully Inn. Ignore a road on the left and in another 100 metres turn left along Ashby Road.

2. In about 40 metres cross a stile on the left and walk ahead through the field to a stile a few metres right of a gate. Cross the

stone bridge ahead and slant right to a wooden footbridge and stile.

3. Bear slightly left towards a line of trees. Before reaching them look for a post that should have a yellow arrow. Go ahead over a footbridge and cross the field to another stile. Keep a watercourse on your left and cross a stile to emerge on the A4055.

4. Bear right and in 20 metres cross the road (with care) to a bridge with railings. Cross the bridge and immediately bear right over a stile. In 200 metres cross a stile at a track.

5. Cross the stile opposite on to an enclosed path leading to a field. Continue to another stile. Walk ahead to a corner and, passing trees on the right, cross a stile next to a gate. Continue ahead, following the hedge and water course nearby on the right. Pass an old footbridge and follow a fence to a stile.

6. Continue on a path enclosed by trees and cross a drive to another path, which emerges in a field. Continue ahead and go through bushes into the next field. Walk on and bear right in the far corner to cross a footbridge and reach the A4055.

7. Turn left and shortly cross the road to follow the pavement in the direction of Dinas Powys. When the pavement ends cross a bridge and, in a few metres, turn right along Cross Common Road.

8. Ignore the road bearing left and continue ahead along the narrower Cross Common Road. It goes uphill, passing two footpaths on the right. About 100 metres after the second footpath, and where the road bears to the right, turn left through a gate. (The footpath signpost may be hidden in the bushes.)

9. Follow the rough track and cross a metal bar stile into a field. Keep to the left boundary and go through a gate into a narrow field. Walk ahead to a stile and enclosed path, which leads to a track, and shortly a lane.

10. Continue ahead on the lane and pass a house on the left.

When you reach a road turn left. In just over 100 metres bear right on a T road. You will soon reach the Church of St Peter, Old Cogan (2).

11. Continue on the lane and pass Old Cogan Hall Farm and a pond. Go through the next gate onto a track and follow it between the Cosmeston Lakes (3). To visit the Visitor Centre take a path on the left to the centre and cafe.

12. Return to the track and follow it to the B4267. Cross and turn right, and almost immediately bear left along St Mary's Well Bay Road. The road descends to the beach at Swanbridge Farm.

13. When the lane ends continue ahead around a barrier, and pass in front of the pub called The Captain's Wife (4). Sully Island (5) can be seen on your left. Your route now depends on the state of the tide.

14. (a) If the tide is out pass the kiosk and descend steps to the beach. Turn right and, shortly after passing the caravans, look for steps that go up into a sports field. Turn left.
(b) If the tide is in walk up the lane and, at the end of the caravan site on the left, go through a gap on to the sports field. Follow the fence downhill and bear right to pass the point where there is access to the beach.

15. If the tide is out you may prefer to continue your walk along the beach. Otherwise walk along the edge of the field and in 400 metres pass the garden of a house (where there is again access to the beach). Continue on a path which passes bungalows, Sully Sailing Club and a school.

16. About 300 metres beyond the school look for a path going inland. It is near a seat and runs between a wall on the right and a field on the left to emerge on the B4267. Turn left and in 30 metres or so cross the road to your starting point at Sully Church.

## Facilities:

Alternative parking in the country park. Pubs at Swanbridge and Sully. Cafe, toilets, Visitors Centre and medieval village in the country park. Kiosk near the beach at Swanbridge, opposite Sully Island.

# Barry *(Y Barri)* – Rhoose Point *(Trwyn y Rhws)* –Rhoose *(Y Rhws)* – Porthkerry *(Porthceri)* – Barry

| | |
|---|---|
| *OS Maps:* | 1:50 000 Landranger Sheet 171, 170<br>1:25 000 Explorer Sheet 151. |
| *Start:* | Car park on the western side of the boating lake at The Knap, west of Barry. G.R. 099664. |
| *Access:* | The Knap is off the A4055, west of Barry Island. Buses from Cardiff and nearby towns. Trains from Cardiff. |
| *Parking:* | Car park above the beach, west side of the boating lake, The Knap. |
| *Grade:* | Moderate – coast and field paths, some road and lane walking. |
| *Time:* | 4-4½ hours. |

## Points of Interest:

1. Barry is an example of a 19th century boom town, which rose from a population of 85 in the early 1880s to 13,000 in 1887 and 39,000 in 1921. The development was due to David Davies, an industrialist who created the Barry Docks and Railway Company. Coal from the Rhondda and other valleys was exported from the newly constructed docks on the eastern side of Barry Island. Day trippers used the railway to enjoy the sands of Whitmore Bay on the southern side of the island. From the 1930s coal exports declined and by the 1950s tourism became important with the development and landscaping of Barry Island as a fairground and holiday centre.

2. The Knap Roman site was discovered during development

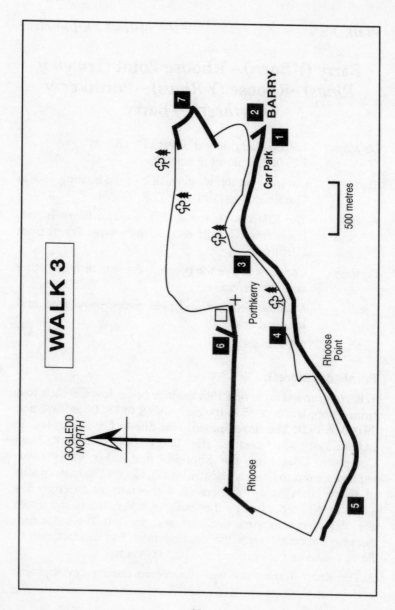

WALK 3

GOGLEDD
NORTH

BARRY

Car Park

Porthkerry

Rhoose Point

Rhoose

500 metres

1
2
3
4
5
6
7

28

work. There are footings of more than a dozen rooms arranged around a courtyard, but the building, which was constructed in the 3rd century, was unlikely to have been a villa. It may have been a military builidng or an official guesthouse. There was probably a harbour to the east in the area that is nowadays occupied by a boating lake.

3. Porthkerry *(Porthceri)* Country Park is a lovely valley behind a pebble beach. A few hundred yards inland the Porthkerry Vaiduct, comprising 18 piers and over 300 metres long, sweeps across the valley. It was built between 1894 and 1898 to carry coal to Barry Docks.

4. The Bulwarks is a large Iron Age hill fort, which may have been occupied into the 3rd and 4th centuries AD. The public footpath goes through the western defences which consist of two banks and a ditch. The line of the path may be an original entrance. When the site was excavated in 1968, three rectangular buildings were found.

5. Aberthaw *(Aberddawan)* was originally two small hamlets separated by the mouth of Afon Ddawan *(Thaw)*. A busy little port, Aberthaw traded as far as the West Indies in the 17th century, when the 'Great Thomas' sailed to St Kitts for tobacco and sugar. Limestone was the main export and the Eddystone lighthouse at Plymouth Hoe (built 1756-9) was built with limestone from the Aberthaw – Rhoose *(Y Rhws)* area. There is no longer a port at Aberthaw and the power station covers much of The Leys burrows, where the port once traded.

6. Cardiff Airport originated as an airfield during the Second World War when it was used as a training unit for RAF Spitfire pilots. In the 1950s the airport was developed for civil aviation use and at first was known as Rhoose Airport. Since then there have been many developments and the building of new terminal buildings, hangars and lengthened runways. Today it is a busy airport and several tour operators start their holiday packages out of Cardiff.

7. Barry Castle is a fortified medieval manor house built by a Norman baron to replace an earlier earthwork castle. His family took de Barri as their name. The ruins consist of a 14th century gatehouse and hall. There may have been a chapel above the gatehouse, which had a portcullis and drawbridge. No walls remain of two earlier stone buildings.

**Walk Directions:**                    (-) denotes Point of Interest

1. Leave the car park at The Knap, east of Barry Island (1), and shortly turn left on a path that rises above the car park. In a few metres you will pass a Roman site on your right (2).

2. Continue with the sea below on your left and follow the path until it emerges at a grassy area. Walk up the left side of the hill and continue along the top of the cliffs. At the end of the grass follow a clear path through small trees and bushes.

3. On reaching a wider path, turn left. It becomes a railed, surfaced path and descends to the beach at Porthkerry Country Park (3).

4. Walk along the top of the beach with the sea on your left. In about 350 metres, where woods meet the beach, take a clear path into the trees. It goes uphill to a field known as The Bulwarks (4).

5. Bear left along a fence and go through the ramparts of the fort to emerge in a caravan site. Follow the left-hand fence and at a corner building bear right and then left to continue beside a fence again, before going up to an access road. (If footpath signs are in place, follow them.)

6. Turn left in the direction of a lower site in an old quarry. When the road turns left into the site, bear right at lime kilns onto the cliffs again. Take care here. In a few paces go left down steps into a disused quarry.

7. Walk through the quarry on a clear path around a cliff edge. The path goes uphill and becomes enclosed by bushes. Emerge

in a field and follow the left-hand fence to a stile. Descend a stepped path to another stile. (Ignore the stile on the left unless you want to visit the beach.)

8. Continue with a fence on the left to a stile. The path now goes above the cliffs with the beach to the left and an extensive quarry on the right. In about 400 metres the path reaches Rhoose Point and a notice with the information that this is the most southerly point on mainland Wales.

9. Continue on the track and pass two breaks in the cliffs. Where the track bends right, walk up to the top of the cliffs again. There is a good view here of the coast towards Aberthaw (5).

10. The path reaches a high fence. Keep it on your right and cliffs above on the left. Descend some steps and cross a bridge. Bear right along a concrete path to a road. Continue ahead over a railway line to a road junction in Rhoose.

11. Turn right and at a roundabout turn right along Porthkerry Road. In just over a kilometre turn right on a lane for Porthkerry. This is the point where aircraft fly into Cardiff International Airport (6).

12. Follow the lane and pass a farm on your left. Just before reaching the 13th century church, bear left over grass to have a wall on your right. Pass a house on the left and take a path into trees. Emerge in a field and follow a fence on the left. Porthkerry Viaduct can be seen on your right.

13. On reaching a stile and track turn left for a few paces then bear right to follow a high hedge on the left. Cross some stepping stones and shortly a stile into a field. Bear right for about 140 metres then go left over a stone bridge. Immediately bear right and in the next field cross a metal bridge on your right.

14. Walk ahead to pass a ruin on the left. In a few metres bear slightly left to follow the right side of a field uphill. Near the top of the field cross a stile on the right. Bear left to follow a hedge

to a stile. Now bear right to a stile in the far corner of the field, near a house.

15. Continue to another stile and field. Slant left to the corner of a wood, where there is a stile. Go downhill with a fence on your right and on reaching the railway line, bear left alongside it. In about 200 metres the path emerges on Porthkerry Country Park drive.

16. Turn left to follow the road and pass a parking area. Cross a footbridge on the left side of the road. In another 100 metres follow a track on the left, which narrows to a path. After crossing a stile, turn right over a footbridge. Follow a path up to a road.

17. Turn left and ignore a road on the right. In 150 metres, just before the ruins of Barry Castle (7) on the left, turn right along Porth-y-Castell. Pass Dingle Close on the left and, in 25 more metres, bear left on a path between a wall and a fence.

18. On reaching an open grassy area, bear left following trees. When the trees stop bear right to have houses now on your left. At the end of the buildings turn left and descend the path of your outward route to the start at the car park.

## Facilities:

Alternative parking in the country park. Refreshments and toilets in the country park. Toilets at the start. Shop in Rhoose. Full facilities in Barry. Mini-golf in the country park. Many attractions on Barry Island including a Railway Heritage Centre. Welsh Hawking Centre. Boat trips to Flat Holm.

# St Nicholas *(Sain Nicolas)* – Tinkinswood – Dyffryn – St Nicholas

*OS Maps:*    1:50 000 Landranger Sheet 171;
              1:25 000 Explorer Sheet 151.

*Start:*      Near the church, G.R. 090743.

*Access:*     St Nicholas is on the A48, west of Cardiff, east of
              Cowbridge *(Y Bont-faen)*. The church is on the
              north side of the village, almost opposite the lane
              for Dyffryn Gardens. Buses from Cowbridge and
              Cardiff.

*Parking:*    Park with consideration in the area near the
              church.

*Grade:*      Moderate – field paths and lanes.

*Time:*       3-3½ hours. Allow more time if visiting Dyffryn
              Gardens on the walk.

## Points of Interest:

1. Neolithic people built Tinkinswood burial chamber for the communal burial of their dead around 4000BC. Originally, it would have been covered by a mound. Being wedge-shaped and with a forecourt, the cairn is of the type known as *Severn-Cotswold*. The huge capstone of local stone weighs about 40 tons and is the largest in Britain. When the site was excavated in 1914 more than 900 pieces of human bone were found. About 40 people had been buried, male and female, of all ages.

2. Three tall upright stones and a capstone are all that remains of St Lythans burial chamber. The height of the stones and the square shape of the chamber suggest it belongs to the type known as *portal dolmen*. The site, which has not been excavated,

33

# WALK 4

St Nicholas

Tinkinswood

**1**

North Lodge

**3**

Dyffryn Gardens

**2**

GOGLEDD
*NORTH*

500 metres

is open and exposed with wide views of the surrounding countryside.

3. Originally called the Manor of Worleton, the Dyffryn Estate was owned by the Bishops of Llandaff for around 800 years until it came into the possession of the Button family. Thomas Button became famous as an explorer when he discovered the Nelson river and navigated the Hudson Straits to reach America. During the 18th century the name of the estate was changed to Dyffryn St Nicholas when it was sold to Thomas Pryce, who rebuilt the house. In 1893 the house was again rebuilt when John Cory bought the estate. He commissioned Thomas Lawson, a landscape architect, to design the garden. On John Cory's death, Reginald Cory, a keen plant collector and horticulturist, took over the gardens. The estate and gardens are now leased to the county council for use as a conference centre and botanic garden. The gardens are open to the public.

**Walk Directions:**                    (-) denotes Point of Interest

1. From the church walk out to the A48 and turn left. In a few metres turn right on the lane signposted Dyffryn. Follow it downhill and in 150 metres cross a stile on the right.

2. Walk ahead slanting left to follow a line of trees on the left. Cross a stile and bear left, but shortly leave the hedge to go uphill to a stile between a gate and a couple of trees. Turn right along the hedge to a stile. Bear left to follow a fence.

3. Leave the fence when it bends to the left. Bear slightly right and walk ahead to a stile in a hedge. Continue ahead to pass the Tinkinswood Burial Chamber on the right. Near a stile there is a kissing-gate giving access to the burial chamber (1).

4. Return through the kissing-gate and cross the stile. Walk ahead, slanting right to a stile close to the right corner of the field. Bear half-right to another stile and keep ahead to the next one. Now slant slightly left to a field gate and then walk ahead

towards trees. Cross a stile and follow the left boundary of a narrow field. At the end of the field pass around a barrier near the wall and walk out to a lane.

5. Turn left on the lane to reach a junction. Go left along a shady lane and ignore another lane on the left. Continue ahead for about 200 metres and then bear right to go through a kissing-gate giving access to St Lythans Burial Chamber (2).

6. Return to the lane and turn left. Bear right on the lane passed earlier. In 700 metres you pass the main entrance to Dyffryn Gardens at North Lodge (3).

7. Continue on the lane for about 150 metres to a stile on the right. Bear half-left uphill to the top left corner, where there is a stile behind trees. Continue beside the right-hand boundary of two fields and then cross a narrow field. Pass under the wires of pylons and follow the right-hand field boundary to a fence type stile at the edge of some trees.

8. Bear slightly left through scattered trees to a stile. A clearer path goes up to a small gate – the stile is about 70 metres left of it. Go ahead following the left side of a field to a stile next to a gate. Continue ahead, bearing slightly right to a stile in a fence and to the right of farm buildings.

9. Turn left and cross a farm track. Follow a left-hand hedge to a corner stile. In another 30 metres, at a post with a yellow arrow, turn left for about 200 metres to reach a wide grassy track. Turn left towards houses.

10. At a seat and waymarked post turn left to the A48. Cross, with care, to a kissing-gate opposite. Follow the right-hand boundary of the field to a corner stile. Go slightly left to another stile. Bear left, but not very close to the fence, and pass behind houses. There are fine views here, to the north. Cross a stile and slant right to follow a fence to a stile on the right. Bear left to a track.

11. Turn left on the track and, before a gate, cross a stile on the

right. In a few paces cross another stile on the left. Bear left and soon go through a gate for Haelfaes Farm.

12. Immediately bear right over a stile. Pass a barn on the left then bear left over a stile. Pass farm buildings on the left and, at the end of the buildings, go through a small gate into mixed woods.

13. Follow the right-hand edge of the woods to a small gate. Go slightly left under the wires of pylons and cross a stile on the right next to a gate. Bear left to follow the left boundary of the field. In 200 metres go left through a gap and follow the hedge to a couple of stiles that are close together.

14. Bear slightly left uphill to a track. Turn left downhill to a junction at houses. Bear right then left to the start at the church in St Nicholas.


**Facilities:**

Tea Room in Dyffryn Gardens. Gardens open April-October daily, weekends only in March. Check for winter openings. Pub in Bonvilston (*Tresimwn*).

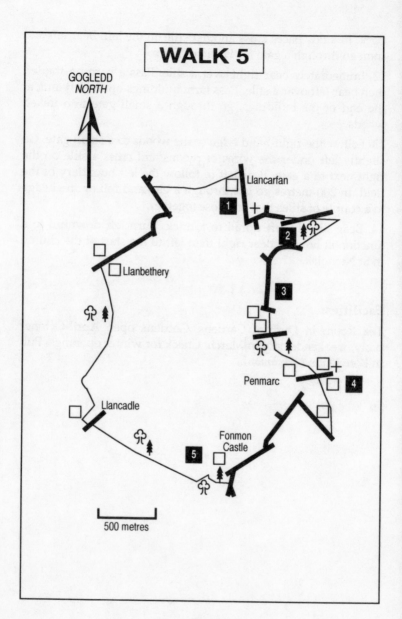

# WALK 5

GOGLEDD
*NORTH*

Llancarfan

1

2

3

Llanbethery

Penmarc

4

Llancadle

Fonmon
Castle

5

500 metres

# Llancarfan – Castle Ditches – Pen-marc – Llancadle *(Llancatal)* – Llanbethery *(Llanbydderi)* – Llancarfan

| | |
|---|---|
| *OS Maps:* | 1:50 000 Landranger Sheet 170; 1:25 000 Explorer Sheet 151. |
| *Start:* | Llancarfan Church, G.R. 050702. |
| *Access:* | One mile east of St Athan *(Sain Athan)* leave the B4265 on a minor road for Llancarfan via Llancadle. Infrequent buses from Cowbridge. |
| *Parking:* | Park with consideration in the village. |
| *Grade:* | Moderate – field and woodland paths, lanes. |
| *Time:* | 4-4½ hours. |

## Points of Interest:

1. Llancarfan was one of the holy sites of Wales. St Cattwg *(Cadog)* set up a monastery here in the 6th century. He was the son of St Gwynlliw, King of Gwent, and St Gwladys, daughter of King Brychan. (Gwynlliw was previously a wicked king, but was converted after a dream and supposedly built a church on the hill where Newport Cathedral now stands. After her husband's conversion, Gwladys became a nun.) Cattwg was educated at Llanilltud Fawr *(Llantwit Major)* and went to Ireland with St Gildas. He also spent time in Brittany *(Llydaw)*. He founded many churches, but his principal monastery was at Llancarfan. It is believed that in the 12th century Caradog of Llancarfan, a learned monk, wrote some of *The Chronicles of Princes*, recording six hundred years of the history of Wales. Llancarfan church may stand on the site of Cattwg's monastery. It is one of the largest in the Vale of Glamorgan and dates from the 14th century.

2. Castle Ditches is a huge Iron Age hill fort with steep slopes below it on the north, south and west sides. The oblong interior is enclosed by a large bank and ditch. It was built about 200BC. There is evidence to suggest a smaller fort was already on the site when it was built.

3. Edward Williams (1747-1826) who took the bardic name Iolo Morgannwg was born at Pennon, Llancarfan. Self-taught and a stone mason by trade, he became a poet and historian. He collected many Welsh manuscripts but, carried away by his fantasies, he added many of his own ideas to the material he handled. A splendid offspring of his imagination was the Gorsedd ceremony, which is now part of the Eisteddfod. (See also Walk 7, end of Point of Interest 1.)

4. The chancel arch is the oldest part of Pen-marc Church, which dates from the early 13th century. There is a later Norman font and a Jacobean pulpit. The yew trees in the churchyard are thought to be 500 years old. In a field behind the church stand the remains of Pen-marc Castle, seat of the Umfraville family. A round tower stands to second floor level and there is some curtain walling.

5. Dating back to the 13th century, Fonmon *(Ffwl-y-mwn)* Castle has seen many visitors, including Oliver Cromwell and John Wesley. The castle is open to visitors between April and September on Tuesday and Wednesday afternoons only.

**Walk Directions:**                                    (-) denotes Point of Interest

1. With your back to St Cadog's Church in Llancarfan (1), turn left. At a fork in the road bear left in the direction of Waterston. At the next fork go uphill and pass the school on your left. At the end of the playground turn right on a narrow lane uphill.

2. Follow the lane as it descends. Cross a bridge at a private road sign and immediately turn right through a field gate. Bear left along the hill slope of the field. As the valley narrows you will have a stream nearby on your right. In the far corner of the

field, take a path descending into trees and cross the stream with the help of stones. Bear slightly right on a path uphill and cross a stile.

3. Turn left and shortly walk through a field. Just before reaching a stile on the left, bear right to follow a hedge and fence on your left to a corner stile. Walk ahead through the ditch of the Iron Age fort (2).

4. Cross a stile next to a gate. The ditch bears slightly left and reaches a fence. Cross a stile and turn right downhill, following the fence. Ignore a stile on the right and descend to a stile next to a gate at Ford Farm.

5. Turn right along the lane to a junction and turn left in the direction of Pennon (3). Where the lane bends left, bear right on a track to have a wall and farm buildings on the left. Pass a house on the right and go through a gate. Descend the field beside a fence, but in 100 metres leave the track to descend to a footbridge in the middle of a valley.

6. Bear slightly right into a wood. Veer left on a path to go uphill and emerge in a field. Slant left towards houses. Where a fence turns inwards between two houses, there is a stile. Walk ahead to the road in Pen-marc. To see the church and castle remains, turn left (4).

7. Return to the point where you arrived in Pen-marc and cross the road. Walk ahead and in 50 metres bear left on a path. Follow it around bends to a field. Go ahead towards the top right-hand corner of the field and pass a house on the right. Walk ahead to cross a stile and emerge on a lane.

8. Turn right to pass the house. Follow the lane to a junction and turn left. At the next junction ignore a lane on the right. Walk ahead until you reach the B4265. Turn right on the grass verge and in 300 metres turn left on the road for Fonmon (*Ffwl-y-mwn*).

9. In about 80 metres cross a stile on the right. Slant left across the field towards the wooded far corner. Pass a marker post and

go downhill to a stile next to an old gate. Cross a stone bridge over a stream and take a path uphill to another path. Bear right through the woods. In about 40 metres leave the path to go slightly left uphill. The path bears to the left and reaches a grassy area near the cattle grid and drive to Fonmon Castle (5).

10. Bear right and use the drive to cross a bridge over the B4265. Immediately go left down steps to a stile. Slant right across the field to the next stile. Walk ahead, slanting slightly left to a stone stile. Continue in the same direction to a stile in a fence. Follow a path between bushes and trees downhill.

11. Cross a footbridge and bear slightly left across a field to a stile. Shortly cross another stile, and in the next field keep to the left until houses are in view. Head uphill to a stile near the houses and road in Llancadle (*Llancatal*).

12. Bear left for a few metres then turn right onto a lane. When another lane joins on the left, bear right between farm buildings. On reaching a field, follow a line of trees before bearing left to the far end of the field. Go through a gate.

13. Turn right into another field. In the third field go slightly left towards trees. Follow a path through the trees and bear right to a stile at the edge of the woods.

14. Enter a field and follow the left boundary. At the end of trees cross a plank over a ditch. Climb a stile and slant to the right, going up the field to a corner. Follow the right-hand hedge to a stile. Bear left and cross the field to a stone stile. Follow the left boundary of this field to a wooden stile in front of a garden. Bear left and quickly right to walk between houses to a gate and the road in Llanbethery (*Llanbydderi*).

15. Turn right and follow the lane to a junction. Bear left to another junction. Turn left and in 400 metres, shortly before the lane forks, bear right over a stile.

16. Follow the left-hand hedge to a stile in a fence. Continue beside the hedge, descending slightly. When the views of the

valley ahead open up, cross the field and follow a right-hand fence and hedge downhill to a stile.

17. Walk downhill and pass a house on the right. Bear right to a stile next to a gate. Turn right and follow the lane into Llancarfan and the start of the walk.

## Facilities:

Alternative on street parking in Pen-marc and Llancadle. Pubs in several villages, including Llancarfan. Fonmon Castle.

WALK 6

COWBRIDGE

Car Park

GOGLEDD
*NORTH*

1

3

2

Llanblethian

4

New Beaupre

6

St Hilary

5

Old Beaupre

500 metres

44

# Cowbridge *(Y Bont-faen)* – Llanblethian *(Llanfleiddian)* – Old Beaupre – St Hilary *(Sain Hilari)* – Cowbridge

| | |
|---|---|
| *OS Maps:* | 1:50 000 Landranger Sheet 170; 1:25 000 Explorer Sheet 151. |
| *Start:* | Car park behind the Town Hall in the centre of Cowbridge. G.R. 996746. |
| *Access:* | Cowbridge is on the A4222, off the A48, between Bridgend and Cardiff. Buses from Cardiff, Llantwit Major and Bridgend. |
| *Parking:* | Car park behind Cowbridge Town Hall. |
| *Grade:* | Moderate – field and woodland paths, lanes. |
| *Time:* | 3½-4½ hours. |

## Points of Interest:

1. Cowbridge was first called this in 1262 and in the 14th century it was one of the largest towns in Wales. It was first settled by the Romans, being on their road between Cardiff and Neath; a Roman bathhouse has been uncovered. The Welsh name Y Bont-faen developed from the time when a stone bridge was built over Thaw *(Afon Ddawan)*. According to tradition, a local farmer hid a cow under the bridge to avoid paying tax for it. The old Welsh name is 'Y Dref Hir yn y Waun' (The Long Town in the Meadow) and when the town was given its charter in 1254 it was called 'Longa Villa'.

The South Gate is the only surviving gateway of the medieval town. The town wall was built in the late 13th century, enclosing about 30 acres. It was over seven metres high and surrounded by a ditch. The West and East Gates were demolished in the 18th century, because of the increasing number of horse-drawn vehicles coming into the town. It is thought the North Gate was a small pedestrian gate giving access to fields.

The Holy Cross Church was built in stages from the 13th century to serve the newly founded town. The central tower is a complicated structure said to have housed a spire, which was destroyed by lightning. The aisles are curiously arranged. Cowbridge Grammar School was founded in 1608 by the Stradling family of St Donat's. From 1685-1919 it was governed by Jesus College, Oxford. The school was famous for its classical education. Dating from 1847, the present buildings were built on the site of the original school.

Cowbridge has many listed buildings. The Duke of Wellington was a coaching inn and originally called The Black Horse, until the Iron Duke stayed overnight and then the name was changed. A well was discovered in the lounge during the 1980s. There is a ghost called the 'Grey Lady' who used to walk along a narrow passage through the building.

The first printing press in Glamorgan was established in Cowbridge by Rhys Thomas in 1770. In the High Street, Edward Williams (1747-1826) kept a bookshop. He is better known by the bardic name Iolo Morganwg (Iolo of Glamorgan). Born near Llancarfan, he worked as a stone mason for most of his life, but was also a poet, writing in Welsh and English. A collector of Welsh manuscripts and legends, he was inclined to make up what he could not find out, confusing later scholars. He was responsible for introducing the Gorsedd ceremony into the present ritual of the National Eisteddfod. He is buried at Flemingston (*Trefflemin*).

There is a museum in the Town Hall, the former House of Correction.

2. Gilbert de Clare built St Quintin's Castle in the early 14th century. The remains consist mainly of the massive gatehouse and a stretch of curtain wall. An earlier keep may have stood on a mound nearby. On the opposite side of the valley, on Llanfleiddian Hill, are remains of a late Iron Age hill fort.

3. Llanblethian *(Llanfleiddian)* parish church of St John the Baptist stands high on a hill above the village. Most of the church was built between the 13th and 15th centuries. The tower was added in 1477 by Anne Neville, wife of Richard III. When the church was restored in 1896 a crypt containing 200 skeletons and pieces of 13th century coffin lids was discovered beneath the south chapel. Near the church there is a small green with the remains of a medieval roadside cross.

4. Llandough Castle is a modern mansion built in a pseudo medieval style. Inside the church there is a tablet commemorating three children who died within a month of one another in 1713.

5. Old Beaupre is a picturesque ruin approached through fields, in the gentle valley of Afon Ddawan *(Thaw)*. It was a medieval and later a Tudor manor house. The original house, dating from about 1300, belonged to the Bassett family and was built around a south facing courtyard. In the 16th century, the northernmost buildings were added, including the outer gatehouse and the most magnificent feature, the storeyed porch. It combines several styles with a Tudor archway and Doric, Ionic and Corinthian columns. It gives access to the 14th century hall with its heraldic fireplace. The ruin is now in the care of CADW and is open every day except Sunday.

6. St Hilary *(Sain Hilari)* is a delightful hamlet of thatched cottages. Inside the Norman church there are effigies and monuments to the Bassett family of Beaupre Castle *(Old Beaupre)*.

**Walk Directions:**                        (-) denotes Point of Interest

1. From the car park in Cowbridge *(Y Bont-faen)* (1) walk out to the main street and turn right. At the Duke of Wellington turn left down Church Street. Pass the church and the Old Grammar School. Go through the South Gate and walk ahead to pass the modern school on your left.

2. When the lane starts to climb turn right through a kissing-gate. Walk ahead on a clear path until reaching a point where there are two kissing-gates. To see St Quintin's Castle (2), go through the left-hand gate and walk uphill through the field to the castle.

3. Return to the path and go through the other kissing-gate. Continue to a lane and bear right. Take a right-hand fork and cross Afon Ddawan (Thaw). Follow the lane uphill and ignore a lesser track on the right. Reach a lane junction in Llanblethian. If you wish to see the church (3) turn right uphill for 200 metres.

4. Walk back down the hill and pass the lane junction where you arrived in Llanblethian. At the next junction turn right. Ignore a lane on the right and continue along Llanmihangel Road. In about 150 metres, where the road bends right, bear left to cross a cattle grid on a track for Newhouse Farm.

5. Immediately turn right through a gate. Follow the right boundary of the field to a stile in the corner. Walk ahead to a small gate at the bottom of the field – it is about 30 metres to the right of a line of trees. Bear left and almost immediately right through another gate.

6. Keep to the left side of the field and keep ahead on a path. Llandough Castle (4) is behind trees on the left. Follow a fence on the left to a gate. Walk between a fence and a hedge, bearing right. Pass an old building on the right and cross a stile. Pass buildings and bear left to an access lane. Turn right to another lane.

7. Turn right and, at the end of a high wall on the left, climb the banking to cross a stile. Follow the wall on the left downhill towards a wood. Cross a footbridge and reach a path junction in the wood. Turn left and follow the path to a gate and lane.

8. Turn right and in 150 metres look for stone steps on the left. Climb a stile and walk uphill to the next stile. Continue through fields until reaching a track near a house. Cross a small bridge over a stream and follow the fence to a lane.

9. Turn left and in 300 metres you reach Howe Mill on the left. To visit Old Beaupre, turn right over a stile. Walk ahead through the fields to the ruins (5).

10. Return the same way to the lane. Turn right and at the next fork bear right and follow the lane for about one mile to a junction in the village of St Hilary *(Saint Hilari)* (6).

11. Turn left and, in a few paces, ignore a left fork. Pass the church of St Hilary on your left and bear left to pass the thatched Bush Inn.

12. Follow the lane downhill and, when the houses end, continue on the lane through woodland. At the entrance to New Beaupre, bear right on a path through trees. Follow the path through the woods so as to pass New Beaupre below on the left. In about 150 metres the path goes left downhill to a stile.

13. Bear right through a small field to a stile. Continue with woods on the right and cross a stile. Walk uphill beside the woods and pass an isolated stile. Shortly bear left away from the fence and cross the field to the next stile.

14. Cross the next field by bearing slightly left towards a corner but, before reaching it, go through a gap in the bushes. Head for the top left corner of this field and cross a stile on the left. Bear right on an enclosed path and follow it to the A4222. Turn left to the Town Hall and car park.

## Facilities:

Pub in St Hilary. Full facilities in Cowbridge. Museum in the Town Hall, Cowbridge. Llannerch Vineyard. Camp site at Llandow, SW of Cowbridge.

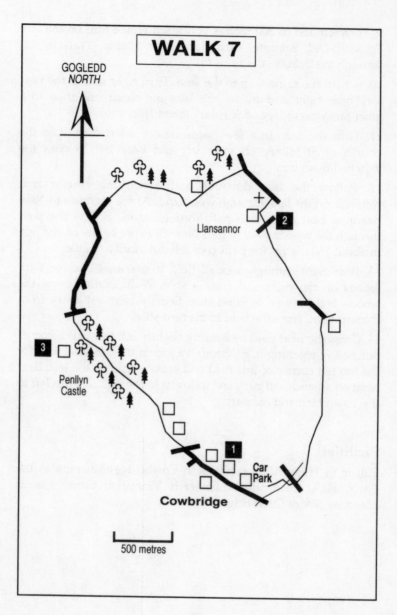

# WALK 7

GOGLEDD
*NORTH*

Llansannor

**2**

Penllyn Castle

**3**

Car Park

**1**

**Cowbridge**

500 metres

# Cowbridge *(Y Bont-faen)* – Llansannor – Penllyn – Cowbridge

| | |
|---|---|
| *OS Maps:* | 1:50 000 Landranger Sheet 170; 1:25 000 Explorer Sheet 151. |
| *Start:* | Car park behind the Town Hall in the centre of Cowbridge. G.R. 996746. |
| *Access:* | Cowbridge is on the A4222, off the A48, between Bridgend and Cardiff. Buses from Bridgend, Cardiff and Llantwit Major *(Llanilltud Fawr)*. |
| *Parking:* | Car park behind the Town Hall. |
| *Grade:* | Moderate – field and woodland paths, lanes. |
| *Time:* | 3-4 hours. |

## Points of Interest:

1. Cowbridge was at one time the most important town in the Vale of Glamorgan, and it was called the 'Capital of the Vale'. It has only one main street, which is on the line of a Roman road. The town may have been the Roman fort of Bovium – the name is derived from the Latin for cow and ox. In Norman times the town developed as a market for Llanblethian *(Llanfleiddian)* castle and it was a borough by the end of the 13th century. It was a walled town; the best preserved of the walls are around the Old Hall Gardens. In the middle of the main road (where Church Street leaves the road) there used to be a preaching cross. It was removed about 1830.

2. Llansannor Court, a 16th century mansion, was owned by Francis Gwyn (1648-1734), who was Secretary of War during the Stuart period, and one of the early members of the Tory party. The church is the only one dedicated to St Senewyr. It has a 14th century east window and doorways, a 16th century

porch, old wall paintings and an old military effigy. Outside there are ancient yew trees and a sundial over the porch entrance.

3. Since the 12th century, when the Normans came to the area, a castle has stood at Penllyn. The original castle was destroyed by Owain Glyndŵr. The Turbervilles, Seys and Stradlings have been associated with Penllyn. The present castle was built in the 19th century, and it is a private mansion.

**Walk Directions:**            (-) denotes Point of Interest

1. Behind Cowbridge (1) Town Hall, walk to the far end of the car park. Head towards the right-hand corner, where there is a footpath. The path crosses a footbridge and continues behind gardens. Bear left under the bypass and keep ahead to cross a stile into a field.

2. Continue ahead, slightly right and, in about 80 metres, at a post with a waymark, walk diagonally left across the field to a stile in a hedge. Walk ahead in the same direction to the next stile. Continue through fields to a footbridge.

3. Walk through a marshy area and cross more footbridges. After some stepping stones bear slightly left to a stile. Follow the left-hand boundary of the field to a path junction. Ignore the right-hand path and climb a stile in the left corner.

4. Bear right to go through a gate. Ignore gates left and right and walk ahead along the right-hand side of a field. Cross a stile and continue on an enclosed farm track. Walk through a yard. Where the track bends to the right, continue ahead over grass to a gate at the road.

5. Turn left and in 150 metres (after a left bend) turn right on an access lane. In about 30 metres bear left to a hidden stile in the hedge. Bear right uphill and go through a gap in the top hedge. Continue uphill to the top left corner where there is a small gate and stile. Go slightly left to more stiles and a lane.

6. Cross the lane to another stile and walk ahead across a drive and shortly reach a stile in a fence. Cross the next field by walking towards the nearest visible house. Before a wood is close on the right, go downhill to a stile on flatter ground. Cross a large field to a stile on the left side of a house.

7. Turn right on a lane and shortly bear left along Court Drive. Ignore a drive on the left and walk ahead to pass the house and Llansannor Church (2) on the left. Bear right along an avenue of lime trees to emerge on a lane.

8. Turn left and pass a drive to The Old Mill on the left. In a few metres turn left on a track and pass a house on the right. Cross a stile on the track and at a junction bear right uphill through trees to a stile beside a gate.

9. Bear left uphill, climbing diagonally across the slope to the high corner of woods. There is a small gate and stile just below the corner. Follow a clear path along the left-hand side of the woods. It descends gradually to a gate. Descend the field towards houses and a stile near a gate.

10. Continue ahead along a lane, and ignore a footpath off it. At a crossroads turn left to pass The Barley Mow on your right.

11. Pass a farm and at the next fork bear right on a narrow lane. When it meets another lane bear right, and almost immediately turn left through gates onto a stony track.

12. Where a hedge on the left bears left away from the track, continue ahead almost to the gate marked Private. A few metres before the gate turn left along a clear track. It descends to pass below Penllyn Castle (3) and follows a high wall on the right for a short distance. Continue on the track through the woods and gradually descend to pass a farm on the left.

13. Cross a stile and bear left up the field to a ladder stile. Follow a left-hand fence for a while, before walking ahead to a kissing-gate in the bottom left-hand corner of the field.

14. Go down steps to a road. Follow the road into Cowbridge and the start of the walk.

## Facilities:

Pub at Penllyn (on the walk). Full facilities in Cowbridge. Caravan and camping site at Llandow *(Llandŵ)*. Llannerch Vineyard.

# Llan-maes – Llanmihangel – St Mary Church (Llanfair) – Llan-maes

*OS Maps:*    1:50 000 Landranger Sheet 170;
              1:25 000 Explorer Sheet 151.

*Start*:      Blacksmiths Arms, Llan-maes, G.R. 980697.

*Access*:     Llan-maes is off the B4265, north of Llantwit
              Major. Bus routes nearby to Llantwit Major
              *(Llantwit Fawr)*.

*Parking*:    On street parking near the Blacksmiths Arms,
              Llan-maes.

*Grade*:      Moderate – field and woodland paths, lanes.

*Time*:       3-3½ hours.

## Points of Interest:

1. Llan-maes is a well-kept small village, lying only a short distance from Llantwit Major *(Llanilltud Fawr)*. The village church of St Cattwg has a west tower dated 1632 and a Norman font. Cattwg is another name for St Cadog, who had a monastery in Llancarfan. He was educated at Llanilltud Fawr.

2. Plas Llanmihangel is a 16th century fortified manor house. In the late 17th century it was bought by Sir Humphrey Edwin who became Lord Mayor of London in 1698. The church dates from the 13th century. Near the church there is a silted up pool said to be haunted by a figure dressed in white. The ghost is thought to be the 15th century heiress and witch, Elinor Ddu. Prone to frenzies, she had an iron ring permanently attached to her wrist. She was tethered by it when hysterical. She drowned in the pool.

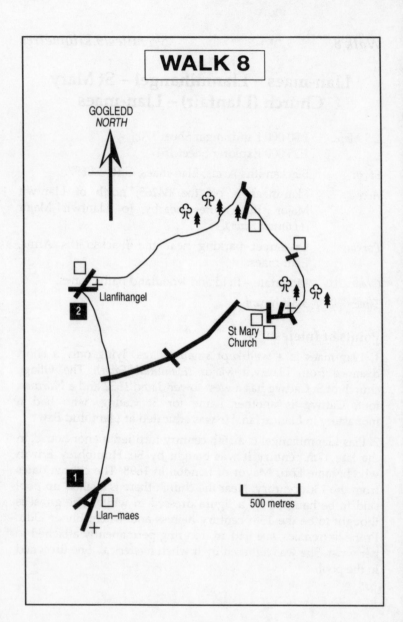

# WALK 8

GOGLEDD
*NORTH*

Llanfihangel

St Mary
Church

2

Llan-maes

1

500 metres

**Walk Directions:**                     (-) denotes Point of Interest

1. With your back to the Blacksmiths Arms in Llan-maes (1), turn right and walk along the road to a junction. Take the road in the direction of St Mary Church (Llanfair). In a couple of paces, before reaching the drive of a bungalow, bear left on a rather hidden, narrow, sunken, enclosed path.

2. In about 150 metres bear left through an opening into a long field. Turn right along the field edge, and in the top right-hand corner go through a gap in the hedge to a stile. Slant right to follow the right-hand hedge to a field gate and lane.

3. Turn right along the lane and, in about 25 metres, cross a stile on the left. Slant slightly right across the field to a corner hedge where there should be a post with a yellow arrow. In the direction of Llanmihangel, walk across this long field to a gap in a hedge near another post. Aim now for the left side of Plas Llanmihangel. Before the end of the field bear left with a hedge on your right. A path descends between tall bushes to a stile at a lane near a bench and crossroads.

4. Take the lane in the direction of Llanblethian (*Llanfleiddian*). Pass Plas Llanmihangel on the left and the church on the right (2). When the lane turns left at the house, keep ahead on a track between farm buildings. In about 30 metres, where the track goes up to a barn, walk ahead to a stile.

5. Continue ahead through the field to a stile near the left corner. Cross the middle of the next field to a small gate at a break in the trees. Bear slightly right, continue ahead and follow a line of bushes and trees to a gate on the right. It is shortly before the end of the field. Cross a stream over a broad, plank bridge into the next field.

6. Turn left to follow the fence, and enter some woodland. In a few paces, at a fork, take the right-hand path. It goes above a small quarry and then descends to a stile and a stony track. Turn left and shortly right to cross another stile.

7. Bear slightly left to cross the slope of the field to a gap in the

corner hedge. Follow a path enclosed by bushes into the next field. Continue along the left boundary of fields for 700 metres to a stile on the left.

8. Follow the descending path through woodland. At a path junction bear right to a gate and lane. Turn right and in 150 metres look for stone steps on the left, going up to a stile.

9. Walk up the middle of the field to a stile near a gate. Continue across fields and, at a track near a house, cross a bridge over a stream. After crossing a stile, follow the fence to a lane.

10. Turn right and, in a few paces, go left up steps to a small gate. Walk uphill to a corner fence. Bear right to follow the fence to a track. Turn left and, before reaching a gate to a house, bear right over a stile. Walk in the direction of a wood. Cross a corner stile into the wood and take the path ahead, ignoring paths off it, and go uphill to a field.

11. Follow a left-hand hedge uphill to the next stile. Continue with a hedge on the right to a stile near a building. Bear slightly right to a gate and follow a track to a junction. Bear right between houses to a lane. Turn left and pass the gate to St Mary's Church.

12. Continue on the road around the church and, in 50 metres, at a gate and path leading to the church tower, turn left on a road. At a junction, opposite Pen-yr-Heol Farm, turn right to pass Pen-yr-Heol Court. Walk downhill and, in about 40 metres, cross a stile.

13. Cross the small field to another stile. Bear slightly right, downhill, to a stile near a gate in the far left corner. Slant left to a stile and lane.

14. Turn left to a lane junction. Take the second lane right, in the direction of Frampton. Follow it for 500 metres to the stile on the right used earlier to cross the fields to Llanmihangel. Continue on the lane for 25 metres. Turn left through the field gate to retrace your steps to Llan-maes.

## Facilities:

Pub near the start/finish in Llan-maes. Full facilities in Llantwit Major *(Llanilltud Fawr)*.

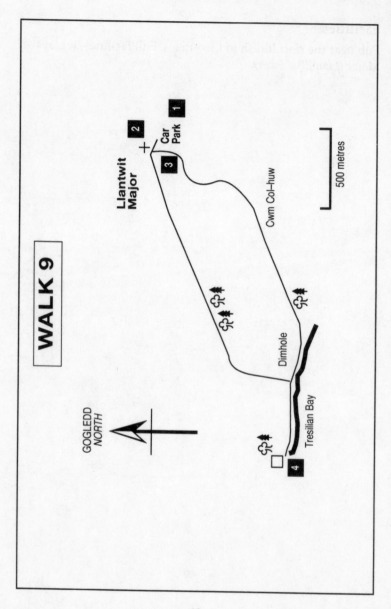

WALK 9

GOGLEDD
NORTH

Llantwit
Major

Car Park
1
2
3

Cwm Col-huw

Dimhole

Tresilian Bay

4

500 metres

# Llantwit Major *(Llanilltud Fawr)* – Cwm Col-huw – Tresilian Bay – Llantwit Major

| | |
|---|---|
| *OS Maps:* | 1:50 000 Landranger Sheet 170; 1:25 000 Explorer Sheet 151. |
| *Start:* | The Old Town Hall (Tourist Information Centre), Llantwit Major, G.R. 967686. |
| *Access:* | Llantwit Major lies south of the B4265, south-east of Bridgend *(Pen-y-bont ar Ogwr)*, west of Cardiff. Buses from Cardiff, Barry, Cowbridge and Bridgend. |
| *Parking:* | Car park near the Old Town Hall, Llantwit Major. |
| *Grade:* | Easy – field and cliff paths. |
| *Time:* | 2-2½ hours. |

## Points of Interest:

1. Llantwit Major has a long history dating back before the Romans built a large villa in a field north-west of the town. Excavations revealed skeletons, pottery and a mosaic floor. The Old Town Hall is medieval in origin and it was built as a court of justice. The nearby Swan Inn was a banking house for Welsh princes. The Welsh name for the town is Llanilltud Fawr, which has been gradually corrupted to Llantwit Major.

2. The present church may occupy the same site as the monastery of St Illtud, which was founded in the 5th century. A Celtic missionary saint from Brittany, St Illtud had many famous pupils, including David, Taliesin the bard and Gildas the historian. This was the first Christian university in Britain. According to legend, there was an earlier church here, founded by Eurgain, daughter of Caractacus (Caradog). It was destroyed by Irish pirates. The present church is in two sections. The west

church contains a number of stones and crosses which date from the 9th century. In the east church, which is used for worship, look for the Jesse tree in a niche near the pulpit.

3. The dovecote dates from the 13th century, when Tewkesbury Abbey had a monastic grange at Llantwit Major. Most other buildings have gone, but this building, built of local limestone, is complete.

4. Tresilian Bay is named after Prince Silian, an early convert to Christianity, who reputedly had a court here. The present house was once an inn, much frequented by wreckers and smugglers. On the western side of the bay, there is a huge cave where a pirate is said to have been buried up to his neck, and left to drown on the incoming tide. The cave has an arch below its roof, known as the 'bow of destiny'. Lovers came here to find out how long they would have to wait before marriage. The number of tries it took to throw a pebble across the arch, without touching the rock of the arch or the cave roof, indicated the number of years the couple would have to wait. Weddings also took place in the cave. The cove has a storm beach, where pebbles have been deposited between the headlands.

**Walk Directions:**                          (-) denotes Point of Interest

1. From the car park in Llantwit Major walk out past the Old Town Hall (1) and turn left. The Old Swan Inn is on your right. Immediately bear left down Burial Lane. Pass St Illtud's Church on the right (2).

2. Where the lane bends right, go up a long flight of steps on the left. On reaching a lane turn left and, in a few paces, cross a stone stile on the right. Pass the dovecote (3) on your right and walk diagonally across the field to the far right corner. Cross a stone stile.

3. On reaching a track (Church Lane), turn left and in 150 metres, go up steps on the left to a stile. Follow the left

boundary of the field to another stile. Bear right into an adjoining field. Follow the left side of this field for a while, then cross it diagonally right to a path running alongside a fence in the bottom right-hand corner.

4. Turn right on a track. Ignore a stile and descending path on the left. Continue on the track with views towards the sea and Cwm Col-huw. The track becomes enclosed, and when a field is ahead, turn left on a path.

5. Cross a stile and shortly join a path that ascends from Col-huw beach. Turn right to follow the cliff path. Descend into a valley (Dimhole) and follow the coast path up to the cliffs again. Walk beside a wall until reaching a point on the cliffs which gives a fine view of Tresilian Bay (4). Steps descend to the stony beach.

6. Return to the valley known as Dimhole, and turn left to take a path rising out of the valley. Cross a stile and turn right to another. Follow the left-hand side of the field to a stile on the left. Continue beside the right-hand fence and, in 30 metres, reach a stile with directions on the wall for Llantwit Major, St Donat's and Dimhole.

7. Cross the stone stile and follow the clear path through a field towards the left corner of a wood. Go over a stile and bear right beside the wood. At a corner of the wood, keep ahead on a clear path. Shortly before the end of the field, bear left to a stile in a wall.

8. Cross a narrow field to a stile, and in the next field keep straight ahead. After crossing a stone stile, follow the left side of the field to a stile. Slant slightly right to the next one. Cross two more stiles close together.

9. Walk ahead beside a hedge on the right to a stone stile in the corner. Continue beside a hedge on the right and cross another stone stile in the wall ahead. Turn left on an enclosed path.

10. The path becomes a lane. Walk ahead to pass the 13th century gatehouse of the grange on your left. At a junction, turn

left. At the next junction, turn right beside the churchyard. Pass the steps used earlier on the walk and retrace your steps to the start at the car park.

## Facilities:

Full facilities in Llantwit Major. Campsite nearby. Public toilets at the start and (slightly off-route) at Col-huw Beach. Kiosk at Col-huw Beach.

# Col-huw Beach (Traeth Col-Huw)
## – Stout Point – Summerhouse Point
## – Col-huw Beach

| | |
|---|---|
| *OS Maps:* | 1:50 000 Landranger Sheet 170;<br>1:25 000 Explorer Sheet 151. |
| *Start*: | Col-huw Beach, G.R. 956675. |
| *Access*: | Take the road signposted Traeth *(Beach)* in Llantwit Major *(Llanilltud Fawr)*, which is off the B4265 between Bridgend *(Pen-y-bont ar Ogwr)* and Cardiff *(Caerdydd)*. |
| *Parking*: | Car park above Col-huw Beach. |
| *Grade*: | Moderate – cliff and field paths. (Take care to keep away from cliff edges.) |
| *Time*: | 3-3½ hours. |

## Points of Interest:

1. St Illtud (see Walk 9) may have landed on a jetty in the creek of Cwm Col-huw in the 5th century. A small port here traded with Somerset into the 16th century. Storms gradually destroyed the structures. About 200 metres from the cliffs are a small number of seaweed covered timbers standing above beach level, which are thought to have belonged to the old pier. A huge delta extends out of Cwm Col-huw, which was formed by the river at the end of the last Ice Age. At that time the river would have been much bigger as it produced the present valley.

2. Much of the land belonging to the Castle Ditches Iron Age hill fort has been lost through coastal erosion, including the original entrance. The fort probably covered twice as much land as it does now. With a sea cliff on one side and a steep hillside

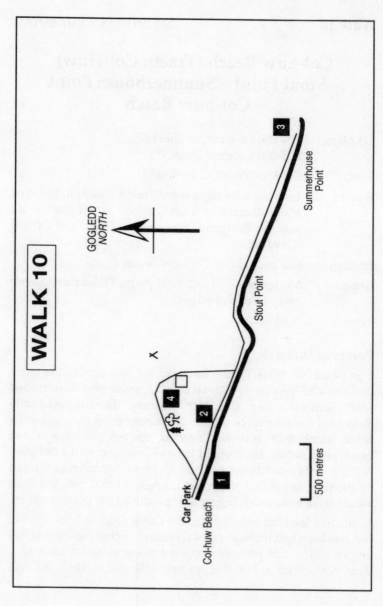

**WALK 10**

GOGLEDD
*NORTH*

Summerhouse Point

Stout Point

Car Park

Col-huw Beach

3

2

4

1

500 metres

66

dropping to Cwm Col-huw on another, the fort only needed man-made defences on the eastern side. The footpath passes through the defences, which consist of three banks and two ditches. The ditches provide a haven for wildlife on this exposed stretch of coastline.

3. Summerhouse hill fort has also lost some of its land to coastal erosion. The coastal path passes through the ramparts and an inner enclosure, which is overgrown. The fort is unusual in having a set of four defences instead of the usual two banks and ditches. The name of 'Summerhouse' is derived from the octagonal building surrounded by a low wall, inside the fort. Now a roofless ruin, it was built for summer picnics about 1730 by the Seys family of Boverton Place. The undisturbed scrubland around the fort attracts birds such as finches, yellow hammers and tree sparrows. Primroses, violets, cowslips and bluebells grow here in spring.

4. As you walk through the woodland of Cwm Col-huw Nature Reserve look for flowers such as red campion, herb robert, yellow archangel, dog's mercury and wild clematis. On the limestone grassland there may be bird's foot trefoil and lady's bedstraw.

**Walk Directions:**                    (-) denotes Point of Interest

1. Leave Col-huw Beach (1) car park by facing the sea and bearing left to a stepped path. Follow the zigzag path to a fence on the edge of the cliffs and go through a kissing-gate.

2. Ignore the path on the left and continue along the top of the cliffs, following a fence. During the Iron Age this field was a hill fort (2). Cross a stile and go up and down steps through the ditches of the fort.

3. Continue along the cliffs and descend to cross a stile. Follow the field edge past Stout Point. Go uphill and along a stretch of open cliffs. Continue along the field boundary to a stile and

walk through a very long field to reach the Glamorgan Heritage Coast Sea Watch Centre.

4. From the building it is only a few metres to the Iron Age fort on Summerhouse Point (3).

5. Retrace your steps past the Sea Watch Centre and Stout Point (3).

6. Ascend the cliff path from Stout Point, and cross the next stile. Immediately turn right. After passing between fields the path becomes a wide track between hedges and reaches a stile near a gate. Walk ahead to a track junction near farm buildings.

7. Turn left and ignore a track going up to buildings. In about 200 metres cross a stile at a gate. Just before the track reaches a lane, go up steps on the left to cross a stile into Cwm Col-huw Nature Reserve (4).

8. Follow the path through the reserve and emerge in a field. Continue through more fields to reach the cliff path above Col-huw Beach. Turn right and descend the path to the car park.

## Facilities:

Alternative parking at Summerhouse Point. Public toilets and refreshment kiosk at Col-huw Beach. Campsite 200 metres from the walk. Full facilities in Llantwit Major (*Llanilltud Fawr*). See Watch Centre at Summerhouse Point. (Check opening times by phoning the Glamorgan Heritage Coast Centre.)

# Nash Point *(Trwyn yr As Fach)*
# – St Donat's *(Sain Dunwyd)*
# – Marcross *(Marcroes)* – Nash Point

| | |
|---|---|
| *OS Maps:* | 1:50 000 Landranger Sheet 170; |
| | 1:25 000 Explorer Sheet 151. |
| *Start*: | Nash Point car park, G.R. 916683. |
| *Access*: | Leave the B4265 at Llantwit Major. Follow a lane to Marcross crossroad. Take another lane south to Nash Point. Bridgend – Llantwit Major buses stop at St Donat's and Marcross. |
| *Parking*: | Cliff top parking, Nash Point. |
| *Grade*: | Easy – cliff and nature reserve paths, lanes. |
| *Time*: | 2½-3 hours. |

## Points of Interest:

1. The Bristol Channel has the second highest tidal range in the world, and this can present difficulties for shipping. Nash Point with its notorious sandbank has been the scene of several shipwrecks. The Frolic ran aground on the sandbank in 1832 with the loss of 40 lives. This tragedy led to the building of the Nash Point lighthouses. Two towers were built 300 metres apart, and positioned carefully for alignment by the ships, enabling them to maintain the correct course. The west tower is not now used.

2. The present St Donat's Castle was built around 1300 by the Stradlings family, and has been in continuous use since then. It is thought the family were pirates and smugglers during the Middle Ages. Sir Thomas Stradling was a Catholic, and tried to hide the fact from the Protestant Queen Elizabeth I. He was

# WALK 11

GOGLEDD
*NORTH*

Marcross

4

5

Nash
Point

**Car Park**

1

St
Donat's

3

2

500 metres

imprisoned for two years when the figure of a cross was discovered in the trunk of a tree which fell during a storm. A gristly tale comes from the 18th century. The Stradling heir, Sir Thomas, went on a tour of Europe with a friend called Tyrrwhit. Before going they signed a pact that if one of them died, the other would inherit his estate. The news came that Stradling had been killed in a duel at Montpellier, and his body was brought back for burial at St Donat's. Suspicion, of course, fell on Tyrrwhit. An old nurse sitting up with the corpse opened his coffin, and she saw at once that it was not the heir; Sir Thomas had a finger missing but the dead body had perfect hands. The real heir never turned up and after many years of lawsuits, Tyrrwhit died. The final settlement gave the Tyrrwhit heirs the castle, but the baronetcy stayed with the Stradling family. Early in the 20th century the castle was sold to William Randolph Hearst, the American newspaper magnate. It became an international Sixth Form College in 1962, and is now known as Atlantic College.

3. The original church of St Donat's dates from 1100 and was smaller than the present church. When the castle was built, the church was enlarged, and again in 1500. The Lady Chapel, built in the 16th century by Sir Thomas Stradling, contains tombs and memorials of the Stradling family. Two calvary crosses are in the churchyard. On the north side is a modern one, but the cross on the south side is 15th century and still has its original head. You can see St Donat's Castle from the churchyard if you look upwards.

4. Marcross church is 12th century. It has a Norman font, a 14th century tower with a gabled roof, and a leper's window to the right of the porch. In the churchyard look for a sundial mounted on the base of a medieval cross.

5. Cwm Marcroes Nature Trail is a circular walk, and a path can be taken either side of the Marcroes brook. The woodlands offer shelter for wildlife, and many varieties of birds may be seen. Keep a look out for scuttling bank voles.

**Walk Directions:**                    (-) denotes Point of Interest

1. From the car park walk towards the lighthouses. Go through a small gate, and bear right to walk on the seaward side of Nash Point lighhouse buildings (1). Pass the taller lighthouse and cross a stone stile.

2. Continue along the coastal footpath, and pass through some woodland. Descend steps to St Donat's Bay (2).

3. Walk ahead, and at the end of the castellated walls, bear left onto a path. Follow the main path through woodland. Pass a field on the left and, after passing through more woodland, cross a stile.

4. In a few paces turn left on an enclosed path. Go through a kissing-gate and follow the left side of the field to a lane.

5. Turn left along the lane. In 300 metres the lane bears right and passes farm buildings on the right. After passing a house on the right, look for a drive on the left which has a long and a small gate.

6. Go through the small gate and follow a road past houses. Continue downhill and bear right towards a parking area. Take a narrow wooded lane that descends to St Donat's church (3).

7. Leave the churchyard and walk about 40 metres back up the lane, then turn left on a wide track. Ignore a left-hand track. Pass a ruin on your left. The track becomes a path through woodland. Ignore a path on the left and maintain your direction to reach a small gate, where there is a farm ahead.

8. Walk ahead to a field gate. Continue ahead and where two lanes meet, take the left fork.

9. At a junction turn left again. Ignore a lane on the left to Marcross Farm. Continue along the road to the village of Marcross.

10. At the crossroads turn left along the lane for Nash Point. Pass Marcross church (4) on the right, and follow the lane downhill until a nature reserve (5) path adjoins the lane on the right.

11. Follow the path through woodland until it emerges in the open. Cross Marcroes brook by stepping stones and, in about 100 metres, recross the stream over a plank bridge.

12. Follow the path uphill to the car park on the headland.

## Facilities:

Seasonal kiosk at the start. Pub in Marcross. Tours of St Donat's Castle in the summer months. Full facilities in Llantwit Major.

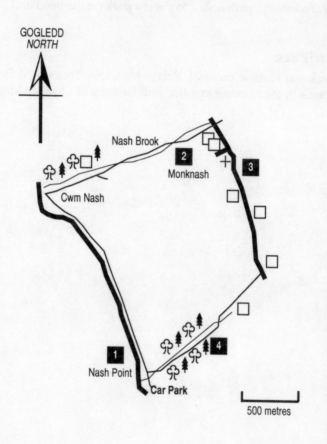

# WALK 12

GOGLEDD
*NORTH*

Nash Brook

2
Monknash

3

Cwm Nash

1
Nash Point

4

**Car Park**

500 metres

74

# Nash Point *(Trwyn yr As Fach)*
# – Cwm Nash (Cwm yr As Fach) – Monknash
# *(Yr As Fawr)* – Cwm Marcroes – Nash Point

| | |
|---|---|
| *OS Maps:* | 1:50 000 Landranger Sheet 170; 1:25 000 Explorer Sheet 151. |
| *Start*: | Nash Point car park, G.R. 916683. |
| *Access*: | Leave the B4265 at Llantwit Major and take a lane to Marcross. At the crossroads go left (south) to Nash Point. Bridgend *(Pen-y-bont ar Ogwr)* – Llantwit Major *(Llanilltud Fawr)* buses stop at Marcross and Monknash. |
| *Parking*: | Car park on the headland at Nash Point. |
| *Grade*: | Easy-Moderate – cliff and field paths, lane. |
| *Time*: | 2½-3 hours. |

## Points of Interest:

1. Coastal erosion has destroyed most of the Iron Age hill fort at Nash Point *(Trwyn yr As Fach)*. There are four parallel banks with three ditches between them, and an entrance on the eastern side. Excavations revealed a burial in one of the ditches. The oblong *pillow mound* within the fort is a medieval man-made rabbit warren.

2. Land around Monknash *(Yr As Fawr)* was given to Neath Abbey *(Abaty Nedd)* in the 12th century, and a grange was built to run the huge monastic farm. All the ruined walls belong to the 12th and 13th century farm buildings. The best preserved is the circular dovecote. To the right, on the east side of the field, stand the walls of the ivy covered great barn, 64 metres long.

3. The small Norman church at Monknash belonged to Neath

Abbey. Its roof timbers are reputed to be from ships of the Spanish Armada.

4. The shape of Cwm Marcroes was formed during the Ice Age by the waters of melting glaciers. Near the sea, the stream twists and turns in loops called meanders. Many types of bird may be spotted along the nature trail, including woodpeckers, chiffchaff and whitethroat. On warm summer days look out for the peacock butterfly.


**Walk Directions:**                    (-) denotes Point of Interest

1. From the parking area walk back towards the lane and, near a barrier on the left, take a wide path descending into a nature reserve. Fork left on a narrow path that crosses the valley. Cross a wide plank bridge over Marcroes brook and walk uphill towards the Iron Age hill fort (1).

2. Cross a stone stile and, with a fence on the left, walk along the cliffs, enjoying fine views of the spectacular coastline. After about a mile, follow the fence as it descends into Cwm Nash (*Cwm yr As Fach*). Turn right along a path through the valley.

3. Cross a stile at a gate and continue on a path through trees, until it emerges on an access lane. Turn left and, in a few paces, cross a stile on the right. Walk ahead for about 120 metres and then bear left over a stile and footbridge. Continue through fields with Nash brook (*Nant yr As Fach*) on your right. In about 400 metres cross a stile on your right and continue above the stream. Cross it at a ford near a wall.

4. Bear left over a stone stile. Walk ahead with the stream on your left. Continue over stone stiles, passing the remains of a dovecote and other ruins of Monknash grange (2). In the last field cross a stile to the left of a ruined building.

5. Turn right on the lane and ignore another lane on the right. Pass the Norman church (3) and a farm on the right, then farm

buildings on the left. Just beyond a farm on the left, look for a stile on the right.

6. Follow the right boundary of the field, and about halfway along it cross a stile on the right. Bear left to follow the fence and, after crossing another stile, pass a house on the left. Cross a stile near a gate and descend to a stile in the far left corner of the field.

7. Cross the stream and walk through the valley. Cross a metalled drive between two gates. Enter the woodland and follow one of the paths through Cwm Marcroes (4).

8. When you emerge out of the woodland cross stepping stones over Marcroes brook, and continue with the stream on your left until you reach the plank bridge crossed earlier on the walk. Retrace your steps to the parking area.

### Facilities:

Seasonal kiosk at the parking area. Pubs at Monknash (*Yr As Fawr*) and Marcross. Full facilities in Llantwit Major.

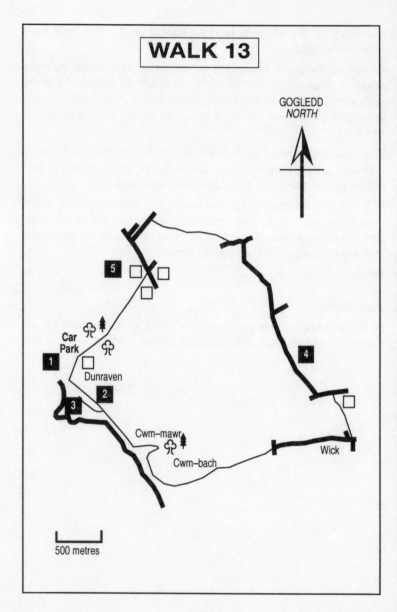

# WALK 13

GOGLEDD
*NORTH*

5

Car Park

Dunraven

1

3

2

Cwm-mawr
Cwm-bach

4

Wick

500 metres

78

# Dunraven Bay *(Bae Dynrafon)* – Cwm-bach – Wick *(Y Wig)* – Pitcott Pool *(Pwll y Mer)* – Dunraven Bay

| | |
|---|---|
| *OS Maps:* | 1:50 000 Landranger Sheet 170; 1:25 000 Explorer Sheet 151. |
| *Start*: | Dunraven Bay, G.R. 884732. |
| *Access*: | Leave the B4524 at Southerndown, south of St Bride's Major *(Saint-y-brid)*. Take a lane to the beach at Dunraven Bay. Buses between Llantwit Major and Bridgend *(Pen-y-bont ar Ogwr)* pass along the B4524 at Southerndown. |
| *Parking*: | Car park at Dunraven Bay. |
| *Grade*: | Moderate – cliff and field paths, lanes. |
| *Time*: | 4-4½ hours. |

## Points of Interest:

1. Surrounded by cliffs 45-60 metres high, the cove of Dunraven *(Dynrafon)* has a large sandy beach, backed by a pebble storm beach. The cliffs consist of Liassic limestone and shale, overlying older Carboniferous limestone. Millions of years ago, earth movements forced the Carboniferous layers upwards, resulting in the anticlines and synclines which can be seen in the cliffs at Dunraven.

2. The walls around the garden at Dunraven were probably built in the 16th century. In the north-east corner of the walls there is an ice house built in the shape of a medieval tower. Ice was cut in winter and stored in straw for use in the summer months. During the 19th century the garden was divided into three by the addition of two brick walls. The gardens contained

vines grown in greenhouses, and an orchard. A herd of fallow deer once roamed the park of Dunraven.

3. The spectacular headland at Dunraven *(Dynrafon)* has been occupied since the Iron Age, and it is said that Caradog *(Caractacus)* lived here. Below the site of the castle, double earthworks of a promontory fort cross the side of the hill. Within the ramparts, shallow hollows and ledges indicate sites of Iron Age dwellings. Lower down the hill, towards Trwyn y Witch headland, oblong, rounded mounds called pillow mounds were medieval man-made rabbit warrens.

Dynrafon was occupied by Welsh princes until the Norman invasion, when Robert Fitzhamon overthrew Iestyn ap Gwrgant, ruler of Morgannwg. Fitzhamon granted Dunraven *(Dynrafon)* and Ogmore *(Ogwr)* to William de Londres, whose son Maurice gave Dunraven to Arnold le Botiler *(Butler)* for defending Ogmore Castle during a Welsh uprising. Although Owain Glyndŵr destroyed the castle in the 15th century, the Butler family retained the castle for many generations. In the early 16th century the male line of the family died out and Dunraven passed by marriage to the Vaughan family, about whom there is a famous legend.

One day, when Walter Vaughan saw a ship wrecked on nearby rocks, he swam out to it with a rope and saved several lives. He worked out a scheme of sea rescue and put his ideas before the government but they were not at all interested. Rebuffed, Vaughan's character changed and he became embittered and wasted his money. He married and had several sons, but the marriage was unhappy. His wife died and his eldest son left home for a foreign land. Another wreck occurred, and this time Vaughan claimed the spoils. It was customary along the coast for ships to be deliberately wrecked by placing lanterns on the horns of cattle. Vaughan took a partner, a wrecker called 'Mat of the Iron Hand', who had an iron hook for a hand. Vaughan seemed to have forgotten that years previously, as a magistrate, he had ordered the seizure of Mat, who lost his hand whilst being arrested. As a wrecker, Vaughan prospered, but misfortune came when two of his sons died on a fishing trip during a storm. Vaughan witnessed their death from the cliffs and turned back to the castle to find, whilst he was absent, his youngest son had fallen into some whey and drowned. More tragedy was to come. During a ferocious storm a ship sought shelter near the coast and, lured by Mat's false lights, foundered. The crew attempted to swim ashore, but only one man survived. There was a rule amongst wreckers that any survivor reaching shore could not be allowed to live. Mat killed the sailor and, recognising the man, cut off his hand. Vaughan was watching on the cliff top and waited as the revengeful Mat approached with the dead man's hand. On one of the fingers there was a ring and Vaughan realised, in horror, that it was the ring he had given his eldest son, long ago.

Broken-hearted, Walter Vaughan sold the manor to the Wyndham family of Gloucester. They made improvements to the estate, enlarged and castellated the mansion, and also extended the garden. Caroline, heiress of Dunraven, married Windham Quin, M.P. for County Limerick. Quin was awarded an Earldom and the family name was changed to Wyndham-Quin. Caroline, the first Countess of Dunraven, extended the house by raising the north and south wings to give another level of rooms. Her symbol is on the pillar at the entrance to the park. In both World Wars the mansion was a convalescent military hospital. It was then leased as a holiday guest house, but was empty by 1960 and quickly fell into disrepair. The owner wished to develop it, but the local authority refused permission, and the house was demolished in 1962. Only the footings remain.

During the World Wars a ghost wearing a light blue dress was often seen at Dunraven. The 'Blue Lady' was considered harmless and always left behind a scent of mimosa.

4. During the spring and summer months the verges and hedgerows of the Vale's lanes are dense with flowers. Umbellifers such as alexanders, hogweed, cow parsley and

hemlock are common. There may be wild roses, yellow toadflax, ox-eye daisies, bindweed, traveller's joy and many others.

5. Near Pitcott Pool there is a well, which supplied the village with water until a piped supply arrived in 1926. Look for ducks and coots on the reed surrounded pool.

**Walk Directions:**                    (-) denotes Point of Interest

1. From Dunraven Bay (1) car park, cross the stile into Dunraven Park. Follow the drive in the direction of the walled gardens (2).

2. Beyond the gardens bear right, or walk through the gardens and exit in the top right corner. Bear right to a fine viewpoint of the coastline and rock platforms. Follow the track to the site of Dunraven Castle (*Castell Dynrafon*) (3).

3. Return to the viewpoint, and follow a low fence on your right. When it ends continue beside a banking to join a fence on your left, and follow it to a stile. Walk ahead with cliffs on your right.

4. The path bears left to a wall. Walk along with the wall on your right to a stone stile. Take a path on the left, which descends gradually into the wooded valley of Cwm-mawr.

5. Cross a bridge over a stream, and follow a path uphill to a ladder stile. Continue along the cliffs.

6. Cross a stile above the next valley, and take the path downhill to another path in Cwm-bach. Unless you want to visit the beach, turn left to take the path inland.

7. Cross a stone stile in a wall. Continue ahead, a short distance from a right-hand fence, to cross the next stile. Walk straight ahead until you reach a hedge. Continue with it on your left. Cross a stile and walk on beside the hedge to another stile and an enclosed path.

8. Emerge on a road and turn left. Almost immediately bear right on a lane to Wick (*Y Wig*). When you reach the village green, where there is a road on the right, turn left on a narrow lane.

9. In about 40 metres bear right through a field gate, and follow the left boundary of fields to emerge where the lane joins the B4265 at a pool and picnic table.

10. Turn left along the B road and in 150 metres bear right along a very narrow lane (4). Ignore a lane on the right and at a junction, opposite Blackwell Cottage, turn left downhill to a crossroads.

11. Turn left and in about 20 metres, at a post with a yellow arrow, bear right. Follow a path around to the right for about 20 metres, then veer left up the banking to a stone stile. Follow the right side of the field to a stile, which is about 80 metres to the left of the right corner.

12. Walk ahead beside a hedge on your right to the next stile. Turn right beside the hedge and, after bearing right around a corner, look for a stile on the right. Turn left and, in a few paces, go through (or climb, if locked) a gate. Follow the right-hand fence and hedge along what was once an enclosed track. Cross a fence type stile on to an enclosed path, and follow it to a road.

13. Turn left downhill to the B4524. Bear left and pass Pitcott Pool (5) on your right. Opposite the car park of the Farmers Arms, bear right to cross the green. Follow a garden wall on your left to a stone stile.

14. Cross the stile into a field and, in a few metres, bear left to follow the hedge to a stile about halfway down the field. Bear right and follow the right-hand hedge. At the end of the next field cross a stile near a gate, and follow the left hedge to a stile in a corner.

15. Follow the fence to a stile into a wood. Walk downhill and, after crossing a stile, continue beside a wall. Pass the Heritage Centre and follow the track to the car park at Dunraven Bay.

## Facilities:

Kiosk and toilets at Dunraven Bay *(Bae Dynrafon)*. Pub on route near Pitcott Pool. Others at Wick *(Y Wig)* and Southerndown. Glamorgan Heritage Coast Centre at Dunraven.

# Saint Bride's Major (*Saint-y-brid*) – Old Castle Down – Ewenni Priory – St Bride's Major

| | |
|---|---|
| *OS Maps:* | 1:50 000 Landranger Sheet 170; 1:25 000 Explorer Sheet 151. |
| *Start:* | Near the church in St Bride's Major, G.R. 894750. |
| *Access:* | St Bride's Major is on the B4265 between Bridgend (*Pen-y-bont ar Ogwr*) and Llantwit Major (*Llanilltud Fawr*). Buses betwen Bridgend and Llantwit Major go through St Bride's Major. |
| *Parking:* | On street parking in St Bride's Major, or on the edge of the common, near the cattle grid, on the northern side of the village (Bridgend direction) on the B4265. |
| *Grade:* | Moderate – downland, field and woodland paths, lanes. |
| *Time:* | 3½-4 hours. |

## Points of Interest:

1. St Bridget's Church in St Bride's Major dates from the 13th century. The large north window of the chancel and west tower are probably 15th century. A recess in the chancel contains the tomb of John Butler and Jane Bassett, who died in the 15th century. St Bridget was born in Ireland and founded a monastery at Kildare. She is also known as Bride and Ffraid. Several places in Wales are named after her.

2. Ewenni Priory was founded by the de Londres family of Ogmore Castle (*Castell Ogwr*) nearby. William de Londres built the present church, and his son Maurice founded a Benedictine

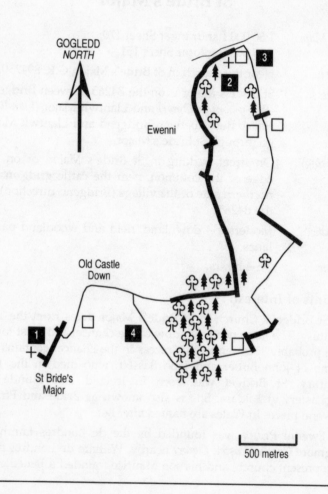

# WALK 14

GOGLEDD
*NORTH*

**3**

**2**

Ewenni

Old Castle
Down

**4**

**1**

St Bride's
Major

500 metres

monastic community, which was linked to St Peter's Abbey, Gloucester. The priory was granted to the Carne family at the time of the dissolution, and Edward Carne built a mansion inside the abbey walls. The chapter house, cloisters and living quarters of the monks have all disappeared, but the abbey church, St Michael's, has survived as a remarkable example of ecclesiastical architecture. The nave has the rounded arches and circular piers of the early Norman period. Of later date are the more elaborate chancel and south transept, which has monuments to Maurice de Londres and the Carne family. The north transept was demolished in the 19th century. The monastery is unusual in having high precinct walls defended with gatehouses, towers, wall walks and battlements. These were built in the 12th and 13th centuries. It is not clear why this small monastery felt the need for such strong defences. To add to the puzzle, the vulnerable eastern wall was much lower.

3. The fields between Ewenni and Bridgend are said to be haunted by a ghost known as The White Lady. According to the legend, she always looked sad and people thought she was in torment over missing buried treasure. A man crossing the misty fields one day spotted her and asked if he could help. She begged him to hold her tightly by both wrists and not to let go until she asked him. He tried to do as she asked but, startled by a dog's bark, he released her. Angry, she screamed that she would be bound for another seven years and vanished.

4. Old Castle Down was probably defended by the Celts against the Roman invaders. Nearby at Castle-yr-Alun graves of the first century AD have been found. They contained two decorated helmets, iron spears and daggers.

**Walk Directions:**                    (-) denotes Point of Interest

1. Starting near the church (1), follow the B4265 in the direction of Bridgend *(Pen-y-bont ar Ogwr)*. In 200 metres go through a

gate to pass a cattle grid, and bear right to walk uphill over grass. In 100 metres turn left on a path. It joins a track on the right. Continue ahead with a wall on the right.

2. Where the track bends right to a house, go ahead. Stay on the track nearest the wall and walk up to a wall corner on Old Castle Down. Bear right to follow the wall downhill.

3. In 300 metres a hedge curves away to the right. Continue ahead to meet it at the next corner. At a fork in the track (where there is an old quarry gate and fence on the left) take the left-hand fork.

4. In 100 metres look on the left for a path heading towards the quarry fence. Follow it and bear right to have the fence on your left. The path descends with great views of Cwm Alun below. In about 200 metres the path bends left beside a fence and emerges on a track. Follow the track through a small gate and go under a railway line. Bear right to a lane.

5. Turn left and cross the stepping stones at a ford across Afon Alun. Follow this lovely wooded lane to a junction. Turn left uphill and then descend to a crossroads. Cross the road and take a narrow lane called Stony Lane.

6. When the lane reaches the B4524 turn left and almost immediately right along Tingle Lane. Turn right at a junction and pass Ewenni Priory (2) on the right.

7. Continue towards a house. Follow the track to the right, and when it ends go ahead on a clear path through a field (3). At the end of the field cross a stile, and shortly a stone bridge. The path, now enclosed, leads to the B4524.

8. Cross directly to a stone stile and a path between houses. Cross a road and continue on an enclosed path to a kissing-gate. Walk uphill between fences to another gate. Continue ahead and cross an old field boundary.

9. Continue to a corner hedge and follow the left side of the field through a gap. Walk ahead and at a gap in the left-hand

banking and vegetation, move over to the left and follow a fence uphill. Reach the lane by crossing a stile to the right of a field gate.

10. Turn left along the road and pass an old farmhouse and barn on the right. In another 100 metres, before the road bends right, turn right at a bridleway sign and walk beside a left-hand hedge through a field.

11. Go through a gate and continue beside a left-hand hedge to a corner. Here, go ahead through a gap in the hedge and walk ahead on an old, rather overgrown track. In about 200 metres it emerges in another field. Walk ahead beside the left boundary to a bridleway sign.

12. Immediately bear left on an enclosed path. In 400 metres it emerges on a lane. Turn right to a lane junction, near a farm. Turn left, and in about 40 metres go up the banking on the right to a stone stile.

13. Cross a small field to a gate near buildings. Slant left to follow a left-hand fence down a long field to a corner stile. Walk ahead on the track and continue through a narrow field to a gate.

14. Follow the right-edge of the field to a gate. Take the path downhill through woodland. Cross a railway line to a path and stile. Slant left across a field to the next stile. Continue on a path downhill to a long stone bridge over Afon Alun.

15. Turn right on the lane and in about 60 metres, just beyond the point where the lane bends right, go left on a clear path uphill into woodland. Go through a gate and walk ahead with a wall on the left. In 100 metres, ignore a left-hand fork.

16. Continue ahead and in 350 metres the track joins your outward route on Old Castle Down (4). Retrace your steps to the start at St Bride's Major.

## Facilities:

Pub and shop near the start in St Bride's Major *(Saint-y-brid)*. Ewenni Pottery. Full facilities in Bridgend *(Pen-y-bont ar Ogwr)*.

# Ogmore-by-Sea *(Aberogwr)* – Southerndown – Pant Norton – Ogmore-by-Sea

| | |
|---|---|
| *OS Maps:* | 1:50 000 Landranger Sheet 170; 1:25 000 Explorer Sheet 151. |
| *Start:* | Car park at the northern end of Ogmore-by-Sea, at the mouth of Afon Ogwr. |
| *Access:* | Leave the B4525 at the northern end of Ogmore-by-Sea, where the road bends to follow Afon Ogwr. Take a road to the car park, which is above the beach. Buses from Bridgend *(Pen-y-bont ar Ogwr)* and Llantwit Major *(Llanilltyd Fawr)*. |
| *Parking:* | Large car park above the beach at the northern end of Ogmore-by-Sea *(Aberogwr)*. |
| *Grade:* | Easy – cliff and downland paths, lane. |
| *Time:* | 2½-3 hours. |

## Points of Interest:

1. Ogmore-by-Sea *(Aberogwr)* is a scattered collection of bungalows on a hillside above a rocky shore. Looking north are fine views of Merthyr Mawr sand dunes. A mile offshore in the Bristol Channel lies the notorious Tusker Rock. In the early 19th century it was believed that a ship from the underworld stinking of sulphur and holding the souls of dead sailors sailed up and down the coast. Hovering above Tusker Rock, a ghostly light foretold the coming of storms and shipwrecks. The light was often accompanied by another harbinger, the *Cyhiraeth*. This unearthly noise rose and fell, terrifying sailors and villagers alike, before returning as a scream or shriek. One of the ships wrecked on the rock was *The Mellany*, built in

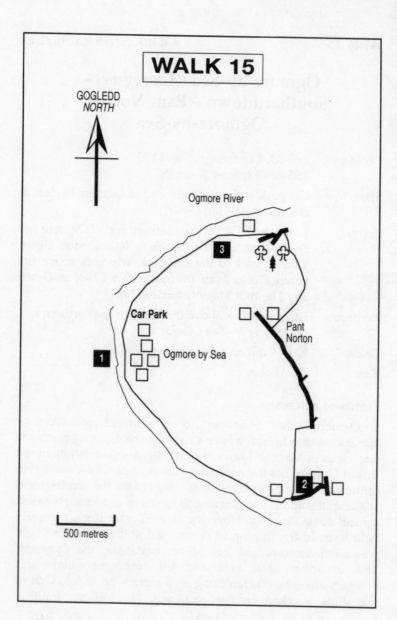

# WALK 15

GOGLEDD
*NORTH*

Ogmore River

Car Park

Ogmore by Sea

1

Pant Norton

3

2

500 metres

Porthmadog, North Wales. *The Mellany* sailed regularly to North America with a cargo of coal. One night when the Captain stayed with his wife in a hotel in Cardiff, they were awakened after midnight by a noise in the room. In the morning they found a mouse had drowned in the washbasin. The captain's wife was going to sail with her husband, but refused after finding the drowned creature. After setting sail, *The Mellany* met a storm off *Lundy Island* and tried to return to Cardiff, but foundered on the Tusker Rock. Everybody on board lost their lives.

2. In Southerndown there is a public house called 'The Three Golden Cups'. The name refers to the coat of arms – three golden chalices on a blue field – of the Le Botiler *(Butler)* family. After successfully defending Ogmore Castle for the absent lord (Maurice, son of William de Londres) Arnold le Botiler was given the manor of Dynrafon *(Dunraven)*. A condition was that when the Lord of Ogmore visited the manor, he must be presented with chalices of wine.

3. Many stories surround Afon Ogwr (Ogmore River). Its waters were once thought to be magical, with properties to foretell the future. Young maidens would soak an undergarment in the river, and carry it home in their teeth to dry in front of the fire. The apparition of the future husband would appear, and not vanish until the garment was turned around. The river was also used as a depository for treasure. If a person died without revealing the whereabouts of their wealth, the spirit would not rest until the treasure was found. The spirit also required the wealth to be thrown into Afon Ogwr downstream, by a living hand. This action freed the spirit from earthly bonds.

**Walk Directions:**            (-) denotes Point of Interest

1. Walk out of the parking area at Ogmore-by-Sea *(Aberogwr)* (1) with the sea on your right. Pass a coastal path sign and a gate

marked 'Emergency vehicles only'. When a wall on the left ends, continue on a clear path, and shortly follow another wall. When this wall ends, walk ahead on a path above low cliffs.

2. In about 400 metres, and at a Danger notice, take a path which rises into a valley. In a few paces, bear right on a path that winds around an outcrop and goes steeply up the grassy cliff. Continue over grass and shortly reach a wall.

3. Continue with the wall on your left. When this wall bends left to a road, walk ahead to follow another wall past a house. At the corner of this wall, bear left to join the road.

4. Turn right along the road, in the direction of Southerndown (2). Cross a cattle grid, and immediately turn left along a bridleway. In 700 metres it goes through a gate, and bears right to reach a lane at a crossroads.

5. Bear left and take the left fork in the direction of Norton. Ignore a lane on the right and, a little farther on, a footpath. After passing the village sign for Norton, and a few metres before a cottage on the right, bear right down a bank to a bridleway.

6. Go through a gate and walk down Pant Norton, a dry valley. Stay on the main track, and at a fork take the track on the right, which rises a little before descending in to another valley.

7. Bear left and follow the track down Pant y Cwteri to the B4524.

8. Cross the road and turn left beside the road. In about 100 metres enter a parking area. Before reaching a house, turn left on a path. Follow it above Afon Ogwr (3), which is to your right.

9. In just over a kilometre, the path emerges near the car park at Ogmore-by-Sea (*Aberogwr*).

## Facilities:

Alternative car parking near Afon Ogwr. Public toilets at the start/end of the walk. Pub at Southerndown.

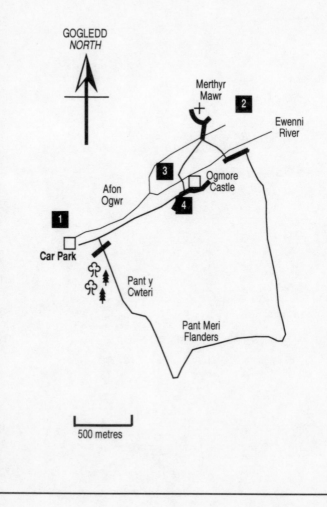

# WALK 16

GOGLEDD
*NORTH*

Merthyr Mawr
2

Ewenni River

3

Afon Ogwr

Ogmore Castle

4

1

Car Park

Pant y Cwteri

Pant Meri Flanders

500 metres

96

# Afon Ogwr – Pant Mari Flanders – Merthyr Mawr – Afon Ogwr

| | |
|---|---|
| *OS Maps:* | 1:50 000 Landranger Sheet 170; 1:25 000 Explorer Sheet 151. |
| *Start:* | Parking area near Afon Ogwr, west of Castell Ogwr *(Ogmore Castle)*, G.R. 874762. |
| *Access:* | The start is on the B4524, west of Bridgend *(Pen-y-bont ar Ogwr)*, between Ogmore Castle *(Castell Ogwr)* and Ogmore-by-Sea *(Aberogwr)*. Buses from Bridgend and Llantwit Major *(Llanilltud Fawr)*. |
| *Parking:* | Parking area on common land near Afon Ogwr, a kilometre west of Ogmore Castle. |
| *Grade:* | Easy – downland paths, lane. |
| *Time:* | 2½-3½ hours. |

## Points of Interest:

1. One of the most macabre legends about Afon Ogwr is the true story of *Cap Coch* (Red Cap). In the 18th century, Afon Ogwr was an obstacle on the road between south-west Wales and London. Stage coaches stopped at the river close to the present-day bypass and the passengers had to walk to Ewenni to catch the next stage coach. Near the river, on a track between Merthyr Mawr and Bridgend, the New Inn provided a welcome stop for travellers, especially packmen who travelled on foot. The licensee of the inn was Cap Coch, who was so named because of his red hair and the red stockinet cap he wore in sympathy with the French revolutionary movement. With his gang of outlaws and smugglers, he attacked lone travellers on the road, and also those who stayed at the inn. Suspicions were aroused when bodies found at the mouth of Afon Ogwr

coincided with the disappearance of packmen. Because there was a market for stolen goods in Bridgend (*Pen-y-bont ar Ogwr*), a blind eye was turned to the coincidence. Some say Cap Coch died peacefully aged 90, whilst others say he was hanged on Stalling Down near Cowbridge (*Y Bont-faen*) for stealing a sheep. The New Inn fell into decay when a bridge was built in Bridgend in the year 1826. In the early 20th century the ruined inn was demolished and a secret cavity was found in the kitchen wall. It was filled with stolen goods. The garden was then dug up, and numerous skeletons were unearthed. More bones of missing travellers were found in the nearby fields and woods. They had remained undiscovered for eighty years after Cap Coch's death.

2. Merthyr Mawr church is only about 150 years old, but it was built on an ancient site, and there may have been a church here as early as 800. Inside the church there is an ancient font. A large collection of early Christian memorial stones have been collected and placed in an open shed on the northern side of the churchyard, behind the church. The church is dedicated to St Teilo, a disciple of St David, who went with him on a pilgrimage to Rome and the Holy Land. When St Teilo returned to Wales he founded the monastery at Llandeilo Fawr in Dyfed, and from there built a number of churches in Morgannwg, Gwent and Powys.

3. The origin of the stepping stones in Afon Ogwr is obscure, but they are at least 400 years old. Medieval monks may have placed them here. Folklore relates that they moved themselves from higher up the river. Another suggestion is that they may have been placed for the use of funeral processions on their way to St Teilo's church. Baptisms have taken place from the stones. They also provide a direct route from the church to the Pelican inn on the east side of the river; public houses are not allowed in or near Merthyr Mawr.

4. The building of Ogmore Castle was begun by a Norman knight, William de Londres, in the 12th century. With the

castles at Coity and Newcastle, it provided the invaders with a defence, and a good base for attacks against the Welsh. The first stone castle was the central keep; it is the highest part of the remains and controlled the inner gate. Additions were made in the late 12th and 13th centuries. A detached building near the farm is thought to be a 15th century courthouse.

There is a legend connected to the castle. Maurice de Londres, son of William de Londres, came to live at Ogwr and he used to hunt in the woods. The disinherited Welsh were no longer allowed to kill wild animals, and anyone found poaching was blinded with red-hot irons. One day, a Welshman of princely descent was caught holding a bow with a dead stag nearby. After being taken to the castle, the following morning he awaited his fate calmly in the courtyard. The villagers and dwellers of the castle had gathered to watch the event, and amongst them was the daughter of Maurice de Londres. The prisoner's proud demeanour impressed her and she pleaded his case, reminding her own people they had taken the land from the Welsh. Because it was her birthday, de Londres agreed to spare the man's eyes. She pressed further, and asked that the Welsh people be given land where they could hunt. Eventually, her father granted the request on one condition – the land would only be the area which she could walk barefoot before sunset. She took off her footwear, and climbed the hillside, pushing her way through thorns and brambles. Although her feet bled, she struggled on, covering as much land as the time permitted. Just before sunset, she reached a point above the castle. Soldiers had followed her, marking the route, which became common land. Today it is known as Southerndown Common.

**Walk Directions:**                    (-) denotes Point of Interest

1. At the parking area, have your back to Afon Ogwr (1) and face the road, then bear left on a path. In 200 metres turn right

on a path that heads towards a valley. At the B4524 ignore a lane rising up on the right. Take the bridleway on the opposite side of the road.

2. Follow the track up Pant y Cwteri. In 400 metres ignore a track to the right, which rises into Pant Norton. Continue through the main valley into Pant Mari Flanders. Pass a well on the left.

3. When you arrive at the top of the valley, you will reach some open ground, where houses are visible ahead, and another track comes in on the left. Turn left across this track, and follow a fence on your left for about 40 metres to reach a wide track on your left.

4. Turn left along this track. In about 250 metres, the fence on the right ends. In a few more metres, take a green track on the right. Ignore a track off it that goes towards a house. In 80 metres cross another track.

5. Head towards a fenced area. Pass a reservoir on your left and follow a green track downhill to a track junction. Walk ahead to another junction.

6. Ignore the first track left, but walk ahead to another green track, which gradually bears left into a dip, and then rises to the fence of a quarry. Follow a line of power cables and continue beside the quarry.

7. Continue on a clear track. At the top of the hill you reach the edge of a golf course. The track descends with fine views towards Merthyr Mawr Warren.

8. At a bridleway sign, continue ahead. Follow a wall on the right downhill to an enclosed track. Ignore a grassy track going into a field on the right, and go ahead downhill through a valley.

9. Go through a gate and follow a walled track. Emerge on a wide track and walk down to the B4524. Turn left for about 150 metres. Shortly before a cattle grid, bear right near a bus shelter and go through a kissing-gate.

10. Follow an enclosed path and cross a footbridge over Afon Ewenni. Slant left across a field to a stone stile and another footbridge. After crossing Afon Ogwr follow the road ahead to a small green near the thatched cottages in Merthyr Mawr. Bear left to visit the Parish church of St Teilo (2).

11. Retrace your steps over one footbridge, and follow a path to the right, beside a wall. The path leads to Afon Ogwr. Cross the stepping stones (3). Walk uphill and pass the entrance to Ogmore Castle *(Castell Ogwr)* (4) on your left.

12. At the B4524 bear right and pass The Pelican public house on your left. Join a path on the right, which crosses a track leading to a water works. In another 400 metres, the path emerges at the parking area.

**Facilities:**

Pelican Inn near Ogmore Castle. Full facilities in Bridgend *(Pen-y-bont ar Ogwr)*.

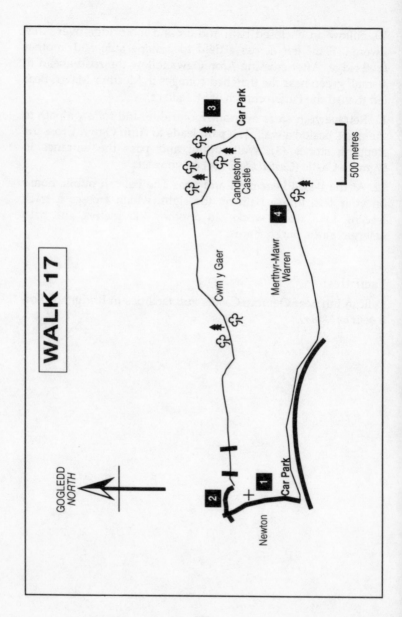

WALK 17

GOGLEDD
NORTH

Newton

Car Park

Cwm y Gaer

Candleston Castle

Merthyr-Mawr
Warren

Car Park

500 metres

# Newton *(Drenewydd yn Notais)* – Candleston Castle *(Castell Tregantllo)* – Merthyr Mawr Warren – Newton

| | |
|---|---|
| *OS Maps:* | 1:50 000 Landranger Sheet 170; 1:25 000 Explorer Sheet 151. |
| *Start:* | Car park above the beach at Newton, near Newton Burrows, G.R. 837769. |
| *Access:* | Newton *(Drenewydd yn Notais)* is east of Porth-cawl, off the A4106. From Newton church, take the road beside the green to the beach. Buses from Porth-cawl and Bridgend. |
| *Parking:* | Car park above the beach at Newton. |
| *Grade:* | Moderate – dune paths and beach. |
| *Time:* | 3-4 hours. |

## Points of Interest:

1. Sandford's Well once had a reputation for healing and magical properties. When the tide on Newton beach is out, the well is full of water. The well is empty when the tide is in. This peculiarity attracted many superstitions, and people thought water taken from the well would remain pure for a whole year. A local physician set up a spa to dispense it. Fresh water from the spring issues through underground fissures onto Newton beach. When the tide is coming in, the force of the flow of water causes the fissures to act like valves. The result is a time lag between the tide and the water filling up the well. At first the well was named after a knight, but it was later dedicated to St John the Baptist.

2. The Church of St John the Baptist at Newton dates from the

12th-13th centuries, when the Normans built the tower as a look-out post. Inside there is a 15th century stone pulpit.

3. Candleston Castle *(Castell Tregantllo)* is a late 14th century fortified manor house, which was occupied until the 19th century. Only the walls remain, but look for a 14th century fireplace on the first floor level of the hall. The name comes from the de Cantelupe (Running Wolves) family, who held the land between here and the sea. It is thought the lost village of Tregantllo was situated in the dunes near the manor house. It was probably engulfed by wind blown sand.

4. Although Merthyr Mawr Warren is privately owned, access is usually permitted, but take care not to cross any fences. This is a Site of Special Scientific Interest, and the dunes are the second highest in Europe. There are six hundred acres of sand dunes. The formation of these began about 4000BC when the sea deposited glacial debris as sand along the nearby coast. It blew inland forming sand dunes against a rocky ridge, and the dunes eventually became stabilised by plants. Marram grass grows near the sea in the most insecure dunes. Farther inland are small trees such as hazel, willow and silver birch. In spring and summer there is a profusion of flowers, including cowslip, rest-harrow, wild thyme, evening primrose and orchids. Look out for butterflies, especially fritillaries. Glow-worms are also present. Fieldfare and redwing may be seen in the autumn and winter months when they feed off berries in the sea buckthorn thickets. A Beaker Folk tomb, containing six skeletons has been found on the warren. Iron Age and Roman tools and ornaments have also been discovered.

**Walk Directions:**                                 (-) denotes Point of Interest

1. From the car park on Newton *(Drenewydd yn Notais)* sea front, walk out to the road and turn right. At the end of the houses, look for Sandford's Well on the right (1).

2. Continue beside the green to the church (2). Turn right along

Church Street and pass The Jolly Sailor on the left. Follow the road as it bears right and, at the end of the allotments, turn left on a wide path.

3. Ignore a path on the right. Walk ahead to cross a road to another path. In another 150 metres cross another road. When the path forks, take the left-hand path. Again, at another fork, take the left path, uphill.

4. Pass fields on the left, and descend slightly beside a wall on the left. Pass two short old gate posts, then a gate on the left. Before the path rises to a fence, bear right downhill on a clear path to reach a flat area.

5. In about 25 metres, bear left on the second of two paths which are close together. In 40 metres, ignore a lesser path on the right. On reaching a small sandy area, go ahead slightly right to join a path at a waymarked post. The path bears right through trees in Cwm Gaer.

6. The path emerges from the woodland in about 500 metres. Here, ignore a path on the right, which goes up a sandy hill. Continue another 150 metres to a junction, and take the right-hand path.

7. In a kilometre you will pass a stone stile and gate on the left. Here, bear right and pass a fence on the left. Descend to a track and turn right to reach a car park. A path on the left goes up to the ruins of Candleston Castle *(Castell Tregantllo)* (3).

8. From the car park bear right to reach a large sandy area. Cross a stream and slant right to follow a line of bushes uphill. Walk ahead, almost parallel to the Ogwr *(Ogmore)* valley, and pass below another sand dune.

9. Continue on a clear path, following a line of trees for a while, through Merthyr Mawr Warren (4). Beyond a marshy area, join a wide track, which eventually runs behind the beach.

10. Follow the track, or walk along the beach, to the car park at Newton.

**Facilities:**

Alternative car park (and toilets) at Candleston Castle. Cafe and pubs in Newton. Campsite off route at Y Wig-fach. Full facilities in Porth-cawl.

# Rest Bay – Sker Point *(Trwyn y Sger)* – Sker House – Nottage *(Notais)* – Lock's Common – Rest Bay

| | |
|---|---|
| *OS Maps:* | 1:50 000 Landranger Sheet 170; 1:25 000 Explorer Sheet 151. |
| *Start:* | Car park above Rest Bay, west of Porth-cawl, G.R. 805782. |
| *Access:* | From Porth-cawl follow West Drive to the car park near the golf club. Buses to Porth-cawl from nearby towns, including Bridgend *(Pen-y-bont ar Ogwr)*. |
| *Parking:* | Car park near the golf club, above Rest Bay. |
| *Grade:* | Moderate – coastal paths, tracks and lanes. |
| *Time:* | 3-4 hours. |

## Points of Interest:

1. The popular seaside resort of Porth-cawl first developed as a port for coal brought down from the valleys. Trade declined when docks opened at Barry and Port Talbot, forcing Porth-cawl dock to close in 1907. A few years later the dock was filled in. There is a small harbour for pleasure craft at the end of the Esplanade. East of the harbour, there are two sandy beaches, Sandy Bay and Trecco Bay, with a funfair and huge caravan park behind them. On the western side of Porth-cawl, the Esplanade and West Drive lead to the springy turf of Lock's Common, and the rocky unspoilt Rest Bay.

2. A tragedy occurred off Sker Point *(Trwyn y Sger)* on the 23rd of April 1947, when the 'Santampa' developed engine trouble and 39 seamen were lost in a ferocious storm. The Mumbles lifeboat, which had been called out, also got into difficulties and lost eight men.

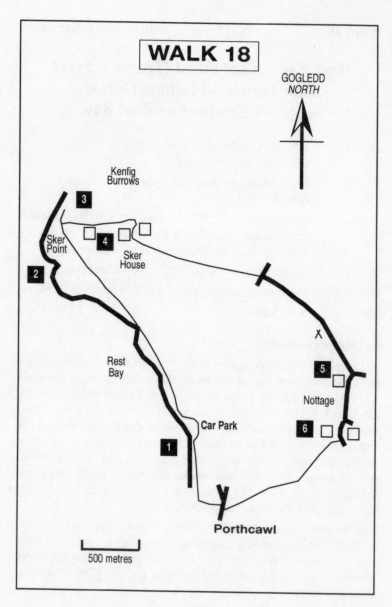

# WALK 18

GOGLEDD
*NORTH*

Kenfig
Burrows

**3**

Sker
Point

**4**

Sker
House

**2**

Rest
Bay

x

**5**

Nottage

**1**

Car Park

**6**

Porthcawl

500 metres

3. The nature reserve of Kenfig *(Cynfig)* Burrows comprises an extensive area of sand dunes, a freshwater lake, and marshes. The dunes are rich in plant life, with flowers such as the wild pansy, burnet rose and evening primrose. Many wildfowl, including swans, visit the pool. To the north, there was a medieval borough with a castle and guildhall. It was gradually overwhelmed by sand, but some remains of the castle are still visible.

4. Sker House was originally built in the 12th century by the monks of Neath Abbey *(Abaty Nedd)* as a manor to live in, whilst they farmed the surrounding land. After the dissolution of the monasteries the de Turbervilles took up residence. They remained Catholics, and Sker House became a meeting place for Roman Catholic priests, who used to hide in recesses between the thick walls. Philip Evans, a Jesuit priest, was arrested at Sker House in 1678, and later hanged, drawn and quartered in Cardiff. Later, the house was occupied by tenant farmers. For many years, Sker House has been a lonely Tudor ruin on the edge of heath and dune, but is now being restored.

Several legends and stories have been told about this lonesome, romantic place. According to one legend, *'Y Ferch o'r Sger'*, a gentleman farmer lived at Sker House in the 18th century. He had two beautiful daughters called Mary and Elizabeth. Elizabeth loved dancing and always attended the *Mabsant*, a festival to commemorate the local saint, which was held in the local town hall. The harpist one night was Thomas Evans of Newton Nottage *(Drenewydd yn Notais)* and, mutually attracted, he and Elizabeth fell in love. Her father was furious – Thomas Evans was only a carpenter by trade. The lovers planned to elope, but the hired coach and horses was heard by dogs, and they alerted the household. Thomas Evans thought it best to retreat. Elizabeth was locked in a room, and later forced to marry Mr Kirkhouse of Neath. She died of a broken heart nine years later, and was buried in Llansamlet churchyard on the 5th of January 1776. Thomas Evans, however, although he pined, eventually married at fifty and had children. In 1819 he died a few weeks after collapsing at a ball in Nottage Court, where he was playing his harp. His burial place was Newton churchyard.

Sker House became famous on the publication of R.D. Blackmore's book 'Maid of Sker'. (Nowadays, Blackmore is better known for another book, 'Lorna Doone'.) The story bears no resemblance to the legend. In Blackmore's tale, a fisherman called David Llewelyn goes fishing off Sker Point, and finds a little girl in a white boat. He takes her to Sker House, where the Evans family look after her. She is the grandchild of Captain Bampfylde in Devon, who is suspected of murdering his grandchildren. Of course, the story has a happy ending.

An upstairs room in Sker House is said to be haunted by the Maid of Sker, who walks about clanking chains in the room where she was held captive. Another ghost is a monk who quarrelled with his holy brothers. He groans during the night. On Christmas morning, a big stone is said to visit the beach near Sker House, for its yearly drink of sea water. There is also the 'Gwrach y Rhibyn', a lost soul who wanders about wailing in the dunes between Sger and Cynfig.

5. The waters of Ffynnon Dewi (St David's Well) are reputed to have healing powers. St David is said to have visited the well, and there was once a chapel nearby. The little valley here was called Dewiscumbe in the 12th century.

6. Nottage Court was originally a farm administered by Margam Abbey. After the dissolution of the monasteries it was acquired by the Lougher family, who rebuilt it in 1570 in the Elizabethan style. R.D. Blackmore (1825-1900), author of 'The Maid of Sker', was the son of John Blackmore and Anne Bassett of Nottage Court. He spent his childhood in Nottage and loved the area.

**Walk Directions:**                    (-) denotes Point of Interest

1. From the car park at Rest Bay, on the western side of Porth-

cawl (1), walk out to the cliffs, and bear right to follow a path beside a wall. At the end of the wall go through a gap, and walk along a rougher path. Cros a beach, and continue with the sea on your left.

2. Cross a stile to follow a clear path. When the wall bends sharp right, walk ahead to Sker Point *(Trwyn y Sger)* (2). Ignore the stile at the gate ahead (unless you want to climb the hill for the view of Kenfig Burrows (3)) and take a track leading off to the right in the direction of Sker House.

3. Shortly pass a pool on the right. The track follows a wall to a stile and fence just beyond Sker House (4). Bear right to pass the house on your right, then turn left to pass farm buildings on your left. Follow a wide track between fields.

4. Cross a fence beside a locked gate, and continue on the track to a stile and gate at a road. Cross directly to Moor Lane opposite and follow the lane as it bears right to pass a farm on the left. In just over a kilometre pass under a (disused) railway bridge.

5. Turn right and pass Ffynnon Dewi *(St David's Well)* (5) on the right. Continue to a junction, and bear right to pass a big farm. You can see the chimneys of Nottage Court (6) behind lower buildings on your left.

6. At a road junction turn left (or bear right to explore the streets of Nottage first). Turn right at the next junction, and take the next road left (South Road). In a few metres, turn right to pass Nottage Forge on the left.

7. Walk downhill and pass a playground on the left. Go around a barrier and follow the surfaced path until it reaches houses. Walk ahead to meet West Drive at a fork in the road.

8. Cross the road and take the left fork. In 80 metres bear left on a clear path across the common to emerge on the cliffs.

9. Turn right and walk along the cliff path with the sea on your left. In 800 metres bear right uphill to the car park.

## Facilities:

Cafe and toilets at the start/finish of the walk. Pubs in Nottage *(Notais)*. Campsite en route in Moor Lane. Full facilities in Porth-cawl. Boat trips. Kenfig Nature Reserve.